In their book *When Hea[ven]* [...]
Tammy Endres have given us an invitation to a journey—a journey of trust until the promise of God is fully realized. The time between the promise and the breakthrough can be among the most difficult times in the life of a believer. Navigating such a season can be one of the greatest trials ever. But these pages contain a road map. This journey is their story, one in which they reveal the issues that have surfaced in their own hearts as a result of believing God for something that is naturally impossible. While it is their story, it is also ours. I doubt there is anyone reading this book who does not have some area in their lives where they are in between the "promise of land" and the "land of promise." Through remarkable transparency Mark and Tammy model this process for us very well. Their courageous story is an offering unto God for the benefit of us all. This book is for every believer, not simply for the one looking for a miracle. By the end of the book the reader's heart will have been searched and brought to a place of greater faith, silencing the voice of disappointment. "Though [the promise] tarries, wait for it" (Hab. 2:3, NAS).

—BILL JOHNSON
PASTOR, BETHEL CHURCH, REDDING, CA
AUTHOR, *WHEN HEAVEN INVADES EARTH* AND
HOSTING THE PRESENCE
WWW.IBETHEL.ORG

I love the way Mark and Tammy have set their hearts to contend for a miracle from heaven. My heart is set in the same way. If your heart is also positioned to seek God with unwavering expectation until He answers your prayer, then this story of their journey will encourage and strengthen your pursuit.

—Bob Sorge
Founder, Oasis House Ministries
Author, *The Fire of Delayed Answers*
www.oasishouse.net

In their book *When Heaven Seems Silent* Mark and Tammy Endres testify candidly about the faith and doubt they waded through after receiving a promise from the Lord. This book can be a great comfort to many who have sweltered in oscillating faith, doubt, guilt, and fear while waiting for their promised miracle. Many well-wishing people have spoken "Christianese" platitudes over such struggling Christians, or worse yet, have said, "Just have faith"—which was no help at all since they already had all the faith they could muster. Christians who have prayed and hoped, seemingly to no avail, and who have suffered what well-meaning friends have said, can find reassurance here. "At last, here's someone who understands, who's been there and still is hanging on in faith." My recommendation? Give this book to Christians you know who are struggling to keep on believing while waiting for their promised miracle. It will help them.

—John Loren Sandford
Founder, Elijah House
Author, The Transformation Series
www.elijahhouse.org

Don't deny yourself the experience of reading this book. It is splendidly written, thoughtfully arranged, and presents a hopeful message to those who have been disappointed by circumstances, conditions, and delayed answers to prayers. Out of a crucible of constantly facing what the world would call a "handicap" and God-given promises of healing, the authors, Mark and Tammy Endres, share with remarkable candor and heart-wrenching honesty the emotional roller coaster that comes with a long wait to see God answer prayers and bring His promise of healing to pass.

Often I find myself wondering where I will stand when I finish the last words of a book. I like where I stand right now, having finished *When Heaven Seems Silent*. I find myself filled with hope and expectation, not with depression and disappointment. This is what an excellent book does!

Mark and Tammy have modeled what waiting consists of—namely, finding the heart of God. They have discovered that the only place to find hope and expectation is right in His great heart!

—JACK TAYLOR
FOUNDER, DIMENSIONS MINISTRIES
AUTHOR, *THE KEY TO TRIUMPHANT LIVING*
AND *MUCH MORE*
WWW.JACKRTAYLOR.COM

When

HEAVEN
SEEMS
SILENT

When

HEAVEN SEEMS SILENT

MARK & TAMMY
ENDRES

CHARISMA
HOUSE

WHEN HEAVEN SEEMS SILENT by Mark and Tammy Endres
Published by Charisma House
Charisma Media/Charisma House Book Group
600 Rinehart Road
Lake Mary, Florida 32746
www.charismahouse.com

Cover design by Justin Evans

Visit the author's website at www.handofjesus.org.

Library of Congress Cataloging-in-Publication Data:

Endres, Mark.
    When heaven is silent / Mark and Tammy Endres. -- First edition.
        pages cm
    Includes bibliographical references.
    ISBN 978-1-62136-661-4 (trade paper) -- ISBN 978-1-62136-662-1 (e-book)
    1. Expectation (Psychology)--Religious aspects--Christianity. 2. Trust in God--Christianity. 3. Providence and government of God--Christianity. I. Title.
    BV4647.E93E53 2014
    248.4--dc23
                                            2014018931

First edition

14 15 16 17 18 — 9 8 7 6 5 4 3 2 1
Printed in the United States of America

We dedicate this book to our daughter, Angela. You have thrilled our hearts from the moment we learned you would be arriving. Thank you for loving us as we stretch our faith to believe that *all* things are possible through Christ. May you and Josh see your "impossibilities" bow to the name of Jesus as well.

Heavenly Father, we also thank You. You wove us wonderfully together in our mothers' wombs, and You set our hearts on seeking Your face. Thank You for saving us and for entrusting us with a precious promise. Thank You for speaking to us and giving us the courage to obey. We are indebted to You for our very lives. It is a joy to trust You.

CONTENTS

FOREWORD

HALFWAY INTO MY flight home from Germany I began reading Mark and Tammy Endres's book, *When Heaven Seems Silent.* Just before landing in the United States, I finished it. I must admit I wiped tears from my cheeks several times.

This is a great book that needed to be written! It is a book written in faith for a promised creative miracle that has been twenty years in the making. It is a book that bares the soul of Mark and Tammy. It is a primer on how to handle disappointment, a primer on how to work through damaging inner vows, and a primer on the grieving process. Mark and Tammy lead us down the narrow road between promise and fulfillment, all while showing us how to avoid the dangerous pitfall of becoming offended. This book is biblical, it is real, and it is moving! For all of you who have a promise and are waiting for the fulfillment, this is the book to read.

I not only highly recommend this book, but I also recommend Mark and Tammy as capable teachers of the Word and ministers of the gospel with strong healing gifts for not only physical healing but also inner healing. I am sure as you read this book you will appreciate the maturity and wisdom revealed in these pages. It makes me so proud to be their friend and to have served as their pastor.

Finally, you will see that one of my spiritual fathers,

Jack Taylor, has endorsed this book. Jack is a well-known author, celebrated Spirit-filled Baptist leader, and dear friend. When we first met in Florida, Mark was with me. Jack told me personally that "the renewal movement does not have a theology for assisting those who suffer. The movement needs to address this issue." I submit that *When Heaven Seems Silent* is the practical teaching we have needed on how to walk through suffering with faith and integrity.

Sit down and read this book with tissues nearby to wipe the tears—not tears of sadness, but the tears that rise up when the Holy Spirit comes and says yes and amen in your heart.

—DR. RANDY CLARK

Dr. Randy Clark is the founder of Global Awakening Ministries (www.globalawakening.com) and author of *There Is More* and *The Essential Guide to Healing.*

FOREWORD

CONTENDING FOR THE promise of God is one of the purest ways of walking with God and getting to know Him. Remaining expectant that God will fulfill a promise He made to us, even if it looks impossible, forces us to place all the pain, grief, doubt, fear, questioning, anger, and incomprehension over our circumstances at His feet and choose worship, trust, and vulnerability to His goodness as our everyday companions. Simeon had a promise from God that he would not see death before he had seen the Christ (Luke 2:26), and God fulfilled that promise. I love thinking about how incredible that moment must have been. In fact, I have a painting and a sculpture in my prayer/writing suite of Simeon holding the Baby Jesus with a look of indescribable joy on his face.

Abraham received a promise that he would be the father of many nations and yet for several decades he was without a son and heir. In hope against hope he believed in the promise without contemplating his own or Sarah's body. He had respect for the promise of God and did not waver in his belief, even though it took decades for the fulfillment. (See Romans 4:18–22.)

God gives us promises so we can become more assured in God's faithful nature and so we can develop a confidence in Him that is so radical it changes who we are in the Spirit. We do not let our circumstances shake our confidence in the promise; we allow it to teach us God's character so we overcome our life situations with what we discover about the Lord's nature toward us.

The promise is designed to empower us to explore the person God wants to be for us. It emboldens us to discover how He wants to move in our lives. The promise upgrades our identity in Jesus. We become watchers of His character and carriers of His Presence. The promise, by necessity, must overcome all the obstacles within us that would keep us from receiving His abiding Presence. The promise then teaches us how to look not in the natural but in the Spirit. We learn the pathway of trust, faith, and glory as we walk by the light of His Word to us.

No matter how long it takes for the promise to be fulfilled receiving a promise from God is a treasure, because learning about the faithfulness of God is one of the most powerful experiences we can have in the kingdom.

—GRAHAM COOKE

Graham Cooke is a prophetic minister and popular conference speaker (www.brilliantperspectives.com), as well as the author of *Prophecy & Responsibility.*

PREFACE

D o you know how it feels to wait for God to fulfill a promise He has made to you? Perhaps you are waiting for a physical healing, and in the meantime you must endure physical pain and face daunting decisions about what to do next. Or maybe you are waiting for financial provision, the mending of a relationship, release from bondage, or emotional wholeness.

Why does God make us wait, knowing it can be so difficult? Why does He make us wait when time seems to be running out? Why does He answer some prayers in a moment and yet fulfill other promises only after waiting for days, for years, or even for decades before the promise comes to pass?

Often God miraculously intervenes without any waiting period, but just as often our loving Father insists on engaging our faith, exercising our trust, and exposing our beliefs in the midst of the wait.

We know how difficult it can be to wait. In our case we are waiting for what some in the church call a *creative miracle*. In creative miracles God makes or forms something that is missing or that was never there. In *healing miracles* God fixes what is already there by restoring what is broken or not functioning properly. Mark was born with a partially formed left shoulder and arm, and only a small bud for a hand. Even those who believe God for *healing* might be challenged to believe He will *create/form* an arm, leg, or hand that is missing.

It might have been hard for us to believe as well, if God had not persistently confirmed this promise again and again, with literally dozens of prophetic words from people around the world, prominent and not, strangers and friends. It would almost take more faith to believe God *wasn't* up to something based on all the confirmations we have received through the years. And yet, we continue to wait. Even as we write the pages of this book, we have yet to see our promise fulfilled.

No matter what kind of miracle you're waiting for, you will likely face obstacles and disappointments at one point or another. Through our journey, we have faced emotional highs and lows. We have wrestled to hold on to faith and trust God's goodness despite what we see.

As you read you will find that much of our story is in my (Tammy's) voice. There are several reasons for this. One reason is that God told me to write the book. When asking Mark to recall how events unfolded, he remembered details but found it difficult to put his feelings into words. Often he would say, "This is too tender and intimate; I don't know how to say it." I assured him that I would get us started and that he could make sure the words accurately communicated and reflected his heart. We are both teachers, but I am a creator, and he is a refiner. God used us together to write *When Heaven Seems Silent*. Carrying this promise has challenged our marriage, but in believing for this miracle, we have also grown closer. As strange as this may sound, when his body is changed, mine will change as well. By a miracle already performed by God, the two of us have spiritually become "one flesh."

The decision to write our story did not come easily, and we would not have attempted it without God's leading. We have depended on God's power and anointing for every word, and we are convinced that He will protect us through times when we may be misunderstood. We have been as transparent and honest as we know how to be.

We are grateful to the team at Charisma House for believing in our story and for publishing our first book. A special thank-you goes out to Wes Harbour for speaking on our behalf and to Adrienne Gaines for inspiring us to dig deeper.

If you are waiting for God to fulfill a promise, we pray that this book encourages you and strengthens your faith. As you begin your journey through the pages of this book, we would like to pray over you the prayer we pray for ourselves:

> *Heavenly Father, maker of heaven and earth, of all that is seen and unseen, we pray that You will proclaim and declare over those who read this book the truth that You have recorded in Psalm 126:5: "Those who sow with tears will reap with songs of joy." In Your name we pray. Amen.*

INTRODUCTION

S HE GOT DRESSED the morning of April 26, 1961, and headed to the hospital with no idea of what this day would bring. Ellen loved her job as a nurse in the labor and delivery wing. She coached new moms through their contractions and wrapped their long-anticipated sweet little bundles in soft blue or pink blankets. Each birth was a unique and happy experience for her.

When word came that Maxine Endres was checking in, Ellen prepared as usual, not knowing that this birth would be different. Maxine's husband, LeRoy, was firmly planted in the waiting room. They wouldn't know if the baby was a boy or a girl until the doctor's announcement. The labor was nothing out of the ordinary. Everything progressed as it should. With the last push came the long-awaited pronouncement: It's a boy! Relief and joy suddenly turned into panic as the doctors and nurses began to realize that something was terribly wrong.

Maxine, still under the effects of anesthesia, didn't realize that Ellen had whisked her baby boy away so the doctors could take a closer look. Something had gone wrong. His left shoulder was malformed, the arm was significantly shortened, and there was only a small bud where his hand should have been. Ellen looked at the precious infant and was left to wonder what Maxine would think when she learned her otherwise healthy baby boy had missing body parts.

Six months later Ellen watched as new neighbors moved in next door. The young mother looked familiar, and soon she discovered why. It was Maxine. Ellen grew to be close friends with Maxine and her son, Mark Steven Endres. Nurse Ellen felt a special bond with this boy whom she had helped bring into the world. She need not have worried what Maxine would think of her son's missing limbs. In time it became clear that neither Maxine nor Mark were going to let his disability keep him from living his life to the fullest.

MEET MARK

My childhood was like any other little boy's. I rode my bike, camped out on the trampoline in my backyard, roughed around with the neighborhood kids up at the public pool, and made it through school with so-so grades. The only difference was that my dad wouldn't let me play team sports for fear that I would get hurt. That was hard because I was great at catching and throwing, and I could tackle with the best of them.

As I moved into my teenage years I felt more self-conscious about the birth defect. I began giving in to pressure to skip school, party, and drink so I would feel accepted by my peers. That went on until my senior year in high school and then things changed.

I needed some help in an English class, and there was a tutor who met with students after school. Little did I know this tutor had more to teach than the rules of grammar and composition. She shared how I could have a personal relationship with God through Jesus Christ using a simple little brochure called *The 4 Spiritual Laws*. I opened my heart and asked Jesus to come in. The change that came over me was immediate and dramatic. I read through the New Testament twice that night. The next day I went to a party but found that I couldn't stay. As soon as I opened the door, I sensed God telling me, "You don't need this to be the person I've made you to be." I stopped drinking and smoking that night.

One of the passages in Scripture that God highlighted to me very early in my Christian walk was John 9:1–5. In this passage Jesus's disciples asked Him, "Rabbi, who sinned, this man or his parents, that he was born blind?" Jesus responded that it wasn't anyone's sin that caused the blindness; it happened so that the work of God could be displayed in his life. Something leaped in my spirit when I read that passage. I knew that I was born with this visible birth defect so the work of God could be seen in me. That realization left me with a joy and a peace that I hadn't felt before.

Though I never planned to attend college, God had other ideas. I enrolled at Southwest Missouri State University and became active with Campus Crusade for Christ's college ministry. I became very good at sharing my testimony. I spoke at events on campus and in churches throughout the community, telling of how Jesus changed my life and how He could change their lives too. My wife often calls me a charmer and a comedian. I don't know if that's true, but I made it a point to approach everyone in a way that would make them feel at ease. People would often comment on how comfortable and confident I seemed to be despite my disability, often adding that they forgot all about my arm until I gave my testimony.

There were times when a young child would point at my arm and an apologetic mom would quietly remind her child that it isn't polite to stare. I would take the opportunity to get down on the child's level and ask, "Do you want to see my hand?" Often the child would ask, "Does it hurt?" and I would explain that it didn't hurt at all. Then I would add, "Jesus gave me a special hand. It's OK." Even though others felt I was lacking something, I felt content and at peace.

Then in October of 2012 I saw a disturbing documentary regarding a drug called Thalidomide. First sold in Germany as an over-the-counter remedy for everything from the flu to insomnia to morning sickness, the drug was advertised as "completely harmless" and "atoxic" during the nine years that it was distributed for human use.

After doing some research, I discovered that between the years of 1958 and 1962 some doctors in the United States had been provided samples of Thalidomide from other countries. Though the drug was not yet approved for sale in the United States, some companies distributed it prior to consent, with the assumption that it would be approved. However, far from being harmless, the ingestion of even one pill during various stages of pregnancy caused severe birth defects, including missing and malformed limbs, curved spines, deformed or missing internal organs, and damaged ears, eyes, and gastrointestinal systems. Many babies died in the womb.

When further US investigations determined that Thalidomide caused severe birth defects in babies, President Kennedy and the Food and Drug Administration banned its use from that point forward. Tragically, an estimated twenty thousand patients in the United States were given the drug, and it has been impossible to know the number of babies who have suffered severe birth defects as a result. Administering Thalidomide to pregnant women has been called one of the most catastrophic disasters in modern medicine.

Since I was born in 1961, this newfound information was unsettling. I was left to wonder if Thalidomide had caused my birth defect. I had some of my birth records, however, these did not answer my questions. So with nowhere else to turn I placed these concerns behind me, or so I thought, and set out to continue loving and serving God.

MEET TAMMY

I was not good at putting questions to rest, at least not when I was younger. As a child I loved the tree house my dad built for my sister and me. It was perfect for a little girl who could climb like a monkey. The rope ladder was a challenge to master at first, but it was well worth the effort as it afforded me the opportunity to pull the rope through the trap door on the platform so that no one could invade my private, leafy hideaway. My dad also attached a bucket to a rope so that I could pull up my paper, pencil, and snack. It was the perfect place to write out my thoughts, something I had been doing since I was very young.

Before I could actually form the words on the page, I asked my mom to write things down for me because I couldn't spell the words I had in my mind. Even at a young age, my thoughts were often about God. I had an insatiable desire to understand God and, more specifically, to understand why things happened the way they did. My determination to figure things out often kept me awake at night. I just couldn't shut down my thoughts.

I came by this characteristic naturally. There were nights when I would sneak into the kitchen for a glass of orange juice only to find my dad in the living room with his own glass of orange juice. We would share the thoughts we were pondering and ask each other questions to dig a little deeper into our ideas of why people are the way they are and what God thought about all of it. When I was fifteen years old I wrote a poem titled "Why" that summarizes the ideas that dominated my thinking:

> It all seems so unfair at times
>   Life has no reason or no rhyme
> I wonder God of Your reason for
>   Making some people rich and some people
>   poor
> In Your eyes we are all the same
>   Yet some of us walk and others are lame
> What reason is there in Your mind
>   That lets some of us see and makes others
>   blind

Sometimes it's hard to understand why
    An old man will live and a young man die
I know it's not my right to ask
    But how do You go about this choosing task?

I remember thinking as a young lady in college that the word *why* even ends with a *y*. And that was the frustration I felt. If I ever figured out the answer to one question that just led me to yet another question. The constant pondering and searching was growing old, and I seemed to be getting nowhere.

After the trauma of a broken engagement and the accomplishment of completing my first year as a special education teacher, I began to attend a church that was a different denomination from the one I had attended as a child. I was attracted to the church because it had an active singles group, but I ended up getting a whole lot more than I bargained for. The sermons the pastor preached focused on having a personal relationship with Jesus, and they always ended with an invitation for people to come forward to "ask Jesus into their hearts." This was new language for me. I had pursued God my whole life and knew that Jesus died on the cross for the forgiveness of my sins, but I had never heard of giving Him control of my life.

All of this gave me something new to ponder. I wanted to figure this out my own way and without feeling pressured. Then a friend told me that there was a book she felt she was supposed to give me. I told her I wasn't much of a reader, and she mysteriously said, "You don't have to read it; I just have to give it to you…so please take it." Well, that got my mind reeling. What was it that I *didn't* have to read?

The book was titled *Beyond Ourselves* by Catherine Marshall, and after reading a few pages I was hooked. The book answered many of my lifelong questions and taught me that *understanding follows obedience*. Catherine Marshall explained that if we understood everything before obeying, we wouldn't be acting in faith. Was it really that easy? Could I gain understanding by simply obeying God? It sounded great, except that the step of obedience He was asking me to take was to invite Jesus into my heart, and I didn't feel ready for that. Over a period of several months the Holy Spirit gently and lovingly taught me what it meant to surrender, and I finally decided to yield to Jesus. Needless to say, a whole new world opened up to me.

Little did I know that five years later, in July 1986, I would meet a man named Mark Steven Endres, and in October of the following year we would wed. I married a man who believed God for big things, a leader who people gladly followed. I had an adventurous spirit myself and was completely in love with this man who studied the Bible more deeply and loved God more immensely than anyone I had known. I felt safe with him and willing to take on anything that God might call us to. But neither of us was prepared for the life-altering promise God would give us and the challenges we would face as a result of it.

*When new information comes
to you, it can be a bit unnerving,
even if it is from the Lord.*

Chapter 1

LEARNING TO HEAR

I FELT SAFE WITH Mark and was willing to take on anything God might call us to, but I did not see this coming. We were heading to a school gymnasium on a Sunday morning...for church. Our one-year-old little girl, Angela, was with us, and we had no idea what to expect. We didn't even know if they would have a nursery at the church or if we would have to keep Angela with us.

The service sounded intriguing when we saw the ad in the yellow pages (there was no Google back then).

Contemporary worship

Casual dress

Small groups

Ministry to the poor

A mission statement that read: *Come as you are, you will be loved*

The church seemed to be everything we had been looking for, yet there was a gnawing feeling in my gut that it was going to be very different from what we knew, in ways I might not like. I suddenly wanted to turn around and head back to the comfortable cushioned pews, hymnals, and Sunday school class that was so familiar to me. Mark, on the other hand, was more curious than nervous. He wanted to be part of a church that reflected more of the values he held dear. In the past we had seen wonderful things happen when we invited friends to our home for Bible study and prayer, but the church we attended was not ready to embrace home groups as an additional option to their primary corporate gatherings. And so we were on the search for a church with a heart for small groups.

The service that Sunday was similar to what I expected in many ways, and I liked it—at first. The worship team had guitars, drums, and great vocals, and the music was uplifting, though I didn't understand why they sang the same verses over and over again. People around us were raising their hands and clapping, which was OK with me as long as I didn't have to do it. And the pastor, Randy Clark, was down to earth and taught the Bible well. All seemed fine until the very end of his teaching.

Randy began to share various physical conditions and/or situations that the ministry team felt people in the congregation might have. He would say one of the team members had a "word of knowledge" that someone had a particular condition or ailment. Then people would go forward to receive prayer from the trained prayer team. The prayer often ended with the person announcing that he was healed of the condition. Now completely out of my comfort zone, I wanted to get out of there as fast as I could. What had we gotten ourselves into? I didn't understand what was going on.

All of this piqued Mark's interest and when Randy called to introduce himself (something he and his wife, Deanne, did with all newcomers), Mark didn't hesitate to ask all of the questions that were swimming in his head. This conversation led to many others where Mark picked Randy's brain. All the while I was unsure and found myself praying that God would not let Mark lead us into something that wasn't from Him.

Then one day Randy invited us to a small group in someone's home. He called the group an Adult Inquiry Group and told Mark that it would be an opportunity to dig deeper and learn more about the values and vision of the local church. Mark couldn't sign up fast enough while I was still worried about what Mark might be embracing.

The group was like a mini church service with worship, teaching, and prayer. People also shared testimonies and asked questions. Randy asked if anyone had an impression during worship. The home hostess spoke up saying she had an impression that someone was being falsely accused of something and that God wanted that person to know that everything was going to be OK. Mark and I looked at each other in shock. Mark managed a supervised apartment complex for developmentally disabled adults, and the mother of one of the residents was falsely accusing him. The woman had been making his life miserable and was even threatening to contact a lawyer. We had not shared this with anyone.

How could this woman have known about this? It was all exactly as Randy had taught and explained it. God let her know about our situation to assure us that He knew what we were going through and was taking care of it. The message came special delivery—through someone who didn't even know us. As a result I felt incredibly loved by God and these people. I also felt an awe that I had never experienced before. Mark put it this way: "The experience took God from way out there to very near." Someone had a message from heaven, and that message was for *us*!

THE FIRST MENTION OF A MIRACLE

We became more and more comfortable with our new church and our new friends. Grateful for how patient they were with our learning curve, we continued to attend the small group and felt that if we missed a night we would be missing out on some wonderful new thing that God was doing in someone's life. One night a woman shared an experience she had during worship. She said that she had wanted to lift her hands in praise but she could not move her left arm. We all thought that was interesting but didn't really know what to make of it. Later that evening she apologized directly to Mark, saying she knew the word was specifically for him all along. She believed that God may want to do something about Mark's arm, but she was afraid to say anything because it seemed so personal. We weren't sure what to do with what we heard but we loved and trusted our friend, so we couldn't blow it off completely.

You would think that hearing those words would have rocked our world. We have tried to think back on what response we gave when she shared her impression from the Lord but we can't remember. I imagine it was something like, "Really, huh? Do you happen to have some diet soda?" The whole thing was a bit surreal but nothing to camp on. We were just opening our minds to the fact that God heals supernaturally—other people, that is. The thought of Mark's condition ever changing had certainly never crossed our minds. Why would it? It was part of who Mark was and living with it was as natural to him as living with his shoe size. The only adjustments I made as his wife were rolling up his sleeve and occasionally cutting a thick piece of steak for him. Then there were those frustrating itches that I had to reach for him, and the few times I trustingly held a nail as he wielded the hammer. We saw no need for a healing or a miracle or whatever it was God had in mind—or did we?

Now it seemed the floodgates were open, as similar words followed over the next several years. The impressions people gave us came to them in a variety of ways. Some heard an inner voice, many had pictures in their minds, some had dreams in the night, and others were reading their Bibles when the impressions came. In most cases people were hesitant and sometimes even afraid to talk with us about their experience because it was so "impossible" that it was difficult to share. Despite this, each person pressed through because they felt they must be obedient to God. Here are just a few samples of what people shared with us privately:

> A friend was reading his Bible and the thought of
> Mark's arm came as he read this verse: "He chose

the lowly things of this world and the despised things, and the things that are not, to nullify the things that are, so that no one may boast before him" (1 Cor. 1:28–29).

A woman we knew had a vision of Mark raising his hands to praise God. She awoke in the night with the vision. Mark was on his knees with both hands raised. He had two fully formed arms.

Another friend had a dream in which she saw a wooden crate and white feathers falling from the sky one or two at a time. She knew the feathers represented prayer. The feathers fell into the crate, and it gradually filled. Two years after the crate was full, Mark was no longer disabled. In the dream our friend felt burdened for Mark because she observed that it was hard for him to keep his focus on God as a result of the miracle.

A dear sister was seeking God for a release of the gifts of the Spirit in her life. Randy prayed for her about this for several weeks. One day she was driving home from work and the Lord reminded her that she had a dream about Mark. In her dream she saw Mark's left arm grown out to the wrist. There was no hand on the wrist, but the arm was perfectly normal. She clearly saw hair on both arms, which was significant because it meant that the left arm was not a prosthetic. Mark was running his right hand up and down his left arm saying, "Yeah, it's OK, we don't have a hand yet, but I expect we will any day now."

One Sunday morning on our drive to church Mark felt that God was telling him to have the children pray for his arm. We had not talked about the miracle for quite a while so this took Mark by surprise. He was concerned that asking the children to pray would make them uncomfortable, and he didn't want to do it. When we arrived at church they announced that this Sunday service was dedicated to the children and that they would all be in the adult service.

During communion one of the children's teachers had a vision of bone growing out. She felt the word was for Mark, and several of the children asked if they could pray. All this took place without us mentioning a thing to anyone about the impression we had while driving to church. Although it would have normally felt awkward, we knew it was God's plan because He had spoken about it before we arrived at church. The Holy Spirit's presence was powerful.

IS THIS BIBLICAL?

It was humbling, exciting, and unsettling to receive these words of knowledge. We had a lot to process. Could this actually be God's plan for us? Could we handle the attention it would bring? Would it happen gradually or suddenly, in a church or at home? Would it hurt? How would our families handle it? But the biggest and most pressing question we had to answer was: *Do we believe this is from God?* We knew it was important to weigh the words given to us, to test them against Scripture, and to ask God to speak with us about it. We searched the Bible, and we each found verses that spoke to us, including this one:

Now to each one the manifestation of the Spirit is given for the common good. To one there is given through the Spirit the message of wisdom, *to another the message of knowledge by means of the same Spirit,* to another faith by the same Spirit, to another gifts of healing by that one Spirit, to another miraculous powers, to another prophecy, to another distinguishing between spirits, to another speaking in different kinds of tongues, and to still another the interpretation of tongues. All these are the work of one and the same Spirit, and he gives them to each one, just as he determines.

—1 Corinthians 12:7–11, emphasis added

It was important to know that the "words of knowledge" we were receiving were scriptural. This passage gave us that assurance.

Going on from that place, he went into their synagogue, and a man with a shriveled hand was there. Looking for a reason to accuse Jesus, they asked him, "Is it lawful to heal on the Sabbath? Then he said to the man, "Stretch out your hand." So he stretched it out and it was completely restored, just as sound as the other.

—Matthew 12:9–10, 13

There is no way of knowing if the man in the passage in Matthew had an arm and hand like Mark's, but every time I hear it or read it something jumps in my spirit. This story brings me to my knees, and I pray that Jesus will soon do for my husband what He did for this man. After all, Jesus Christ is the same yesterday and today and forever (Heb. 13:8).

We were familiar with the teaching in some churches that the supernatural gifts of the Spirit ceased after the canonization of the Bible, or after the death of the apostles, or after the death of the first church disciples. We needed to know whether to believe that for ourselves or not. Hebrews 13:8 gave us the answer we sought. It showed us that it is not unbiblical to expect Jesus to do today what He did when He walked on earth.

These scriptures gave us some level of comfort, but we had a longing to hear God speak directly and specifically to our hearts. God heard our prayers and highlighted a familiar section of Scripture. Mark had gone through several weeks of feeling deeply discontented with his body, which was very unusual. He had not suffered discontentment since he had asked Jesus into his heart because God healed his poor self-image.

Mark was reading John 9:1–12, the story of the man born blind. God had emphasized that passage early in Mark's Christian walk to show him that He had a purpose for his disability "so that the work of God might be displayed in his life" (v. 3). Mark felt so impacted by those words that he didn't focus much attention on the verses that followed.

> Having said this, he spit on the ground, made some mud with the saliva, and put it on the man's eyes. "Go," he told him, "wash in the Pool of

Siloam" (this word means Sent). So the man went and washed, and came home seeing.

—John 9:6–7

Mark was familiar with hearing the Lord through an inner voice, but for the first time he heard the Lord speak directly to him about his birth defect. God spoke by asking a question, "Mark, how was I ultimately glorified through this man?" Mark was shocked when he heard himself respond immediately, "When he was healed!" The passage that Mark had held on to for twelve years now spoke new revelation to his spirit. More than ever, it seemed that the words of knowledge spoken over him about receiving an arm and a hand were from God. The words did not contradict Scripture and the Lord confirmed that to Mark personally and directly.

RECEIVING A WORD OF KNOWLEDGE

God has used our pastor, Randy Clark, to give many words of knowledge to people in the body of Christ and to others who did not yet know the Lord. He gave Randy a heart to equip his local congregation to understand and walk in the power of the Holy Spirit. Randy founded Global Awakening, and he now travels the world equipping the church to move in spiritual gifts. He defines a word of knowledge this way:

A word of knowledge is a supernatural revelation of information that is given by the Holy Spirit. It is not something that the person who gets the word knows by their own senses, rather, it is supernaturally revealed by the Holy Spirit. I can't see someone walking down the street with a cast on their leg and say, "The Lord tells me that you have something wrong with your leg." Something like that would be ridiculous! You can receive a word that God wants to heal that person, but not that something is wrong with their leg. It has to be supernaturally revealed in order to be a gift of the Spirit. Something that is known by natural intuition cannot be revealed by the Spirit.[1]

Just as it is important for us to know how to give a word of knowledge, it is important that we know how to receive a word of knowledge. There are three guidelines that are helpful in thinking through a word of knowledge that you have received:

- Hear accurately
- Interpret objectively
- Apply prayerfully

Let's look at each of these aspects.

Hear accurately

Hearing accurately is not always easy. You might be in a setting that has many distractions. When you have someone giving you a special-delivery message from the Lord, it will often elicit an emotional response. These emotions may actually distort what you've heard. We have found it very helpful to write the words down as soon as possible and to ask others to check them for accuracy. We also have asked the person who gave the word, especially if it came in a dream, to write it out for us. We can accurately recount the words given to us, even though they came twenty years ago, because we kept a journal and saved cards and notes from others. We also have *cassette tapes* of words we've been given (yes, we're that old). Nowadays it's easy to record on smart phones.

Interpret objectively

There are many things to consider when interpreting a word. Please keep in mind that these are not hard and fast rules but general guidelines.

How was the word given?

Mark and I tend to give more weight to words delivered with a humble heart. When a person says he had an impression and that it may or may not be God, there is room for you to decide for yourself. On the contrary, when a word is delivered with a "thus saith the Lord" attached, it can make you feel you have no choice but to accept it. But Scripture tells us to test words, so you should never feel as though you have no option but to accept the word. As a side note, keep in mind that there are sincere believers who worship in a culture where it is common to present words in "thus saith the Lord" terms. They may not be intending to make you feel as though you must accept the word. As long as their hearts are not prideful and their intent is not to back you into a corner, it is important to consider what they have to say.

How do you feel when receiving the word?

Words of knowledge can come as confirmation or information. *Confirmation* is when the giver speaks of something the Lord has already been talking with you about or something you are seeking answers for. You will usually feel in awe of the fact that God has revealed your situation to this person who knew nothing about it. This can be very reassuring.

Information is when the giver speaks of something new, something you have never considered. You will usually feel surprised and a bit overwhelmed, possibly excited. Some will tell you that the number one measure of whether a word of knowledge is from the Lord is that you will feel peace. This is true, but the peace may not be instantaneous. When new information comes to you, it can be a bit unnerving, even if it is from the Lord. Peace should come eventually, and your spirit will settle in, but it may take some time.

We think the number one indication that a word is from the Lord is that you feel (sense, experience, encounter) God's presence at the time of the delivery. You might experience feelings of awe, reverence, glory, joy, laughter, tears, and/or peace. You may also experience physical responses such as shaking, heat, or falling prostrate. These are not the only ways to be aware of God's presence, but they are some of the most common experiences we have observed.

Graham Cooke speaks of this in his book *Prophecy & Responsibility*:

> People who get hung up on accuracy and content before weighing the spirit of the word are liable to

make huge mistakes. We need to do both. In spiritual things, we understand with our mind but know in our spirit. "For who among men knows the thoughts of a man except the spirit of the man which is in him? Even so the thoughts of God no one knows except the Spirit of God," Paul wrote in 1 Corinthians 2:11–12. "Now we have received, not the spirit of the world, but the Spirit who is from God, so that we may know the things freely given to us by God." We just know in our knower, as the cliché goes. Sometimes, we cannot even explain it to someone else. There are times when our intuition doesn't make sense but we still need to listen to it.[2]

Does the word of knowledge contradict Scripture?

It is safe to say that a word of knowledge that is from the Lord will not contradict what the Bible says. However, we need to recognize that God often gives clarity to our perspective or correction to our interpretation of His Word. For example, if a believer is open, God will correct the interpretation that says prophetic gifts are no longer for the church today. It is also important to realize that God may speak a word to you that you cannot find a specific chapter and verse to confirm. For instance, you may hear from the Lord that you are to marry the person you are dating. You will not find a specific name and date in the Bible, but you will find that marriage is God's idea and that He directs your steps and gives you wisdom when you ask Him.

Graham Cooke also states:

Our lives are built on Scripture, not on prophecy. In the event of a clash between a word and the Bible, we must always abandon the prophecy in favour of Scripture, the revealed Word of God. We must be especially careful that the substance of the extra-biblical revelation does not contradict the Bible, but is in accord with the revealed message.[3]

Apply prayerfully

Just as it is important to hear a word of knowledge accurately and to interpret the word of knowledge objectively, it is also important to apply the word of knowledge prayerfully. The purpose of a word of knowledge is to increase faith in both the person praying and the person receiving prayer. God puts us in the position where we have to engage our faith. If the word of knowledge is for healing then prayer can go up for the healing with a level of faith that may not have been as strong if the word had not been given.

It does not mean that the person in need of healing should throw away all her medication. The word of knowledge jump starts a process. Sometimes there is a complete and instant healing, while other times the healing process begins but is completed over a period of time. Pertinent information from your doctor should be the basis of decisions you make after receiving prayer. If you are seeing a doctor, let him know you have received a healing and his confirmation can serve as an additional testimony and credible confirmation that a miracle has taken place.

The same is true for other types of words of knowledge.

A person may have an impression that there is a job change and geographic move in his future. That does not mean he should quit his job and put his house on the market the next day. As stated earlier, the word of knowledge may be confirmation of something you've been speaking to God about or it may be new information. Either way, it is an invitation to press in to God with a deeper level of faith. God will make provision over time, doors will open and close, and the words spoken, if they truly were of the Lord, will come to pass.

Someone once gave us a word about a geographic move. At the time we had a neighbor who got violently drunk on a regular basis, which was unnerving because Mark was traveling a lot. We were excited that God might move us to a safer location in St. Louis. That didn't happen, but three years later the Lord led us to move to Colorado where we lived in an apartment. Soon after, we recognized that the apartment matched the description given in the word of knowledge. How fun and confirming!

Sometimes a word of knowledge is encouraging and exactly what you want to hear. Receiving the word without first asking God about it is a temptation, but be sure to ask God to confirm the word or to speak to you further about it. Remember, the person giving and the person receiving the word can make mistakes. You are more likely to apply the word correctly if you run it by the One who is perfect and is never uncertain about His plans for you.

DON'T FORGET

- *Hear accurately:* Take notes or record what people say to you when they give you a word of knowledge.

- *Interpret objectively:* Was the person speaking out of empathy or from the Holy Spirit? Did they demonstrate humility? Did you sense God's presence? Does the word align with or contradict Scripture, the revealed Word of God?

- *Apply prayerfully:* Do not move ahead on a word until God says it's time and opens a door, or until you know He is giving you a choice on how to respond.

LET'S PRAY

Father, I'm so very grateful that You want to speak to me. Help me to receive from others when their words are from You. Help me to let go of words that are not from You and to know the difference between the two. Don't ever let me disregard a word just because it makes me uncomfortable. I commit to seeking direction from You. I want to hold on to what I should hold on to without fear. Never allow me to run ahead of You and do not let me lag behind. I trust You Lord. Amen.

There is a time to rest in quietness and a time to fight in confidence, but how do we know what it's time for now? We know by asking God and listening for His direction.

Chapter 2

HOLDING ON TO HOPE

COULDN'T BELIEVE WE were actually doing this. When the flyer arrived at the church office, my heart skipped a beat. John Wimber was hosting a healing conference in Anaheim, California. John had an incredibly anointed healing ministry. In fact, Randy Clark learned much of what he was teaching on healing directly from John. We had read John's books, one of which briefly discusses Randy's local church, and we wanted to attend the conference in Anaheim, especially since we were carrying a promise for a creative miracle.

The only thing left to figure out now was how to afford the trip to California so that we could get to the place of our miracle. Then out of the blue a check came in the mail. My aunt was giving each of her nieces and nephews $500. We were certain it was God's provision for us to go to Anaheim and receive an arm and a hand for Mark. Once we decided we were going, more provision began to pour in. Someone offered us a home to stay in, and another person offered us a car to use, all free of charge. More convinced than ever, we made arrangements for a friend to watch our daughter, and we boarded the plane.

It was a blessing to have our home group leaders go

with us. I'll never forget the rush of excitement I felt when we walked into the huge auditorium with the worship band warming up and the sheer white drapes in the background. If you had asked me, as I took my seat, if this would be God's timing for our miracle, I would have said, "It may or may not be." After all, that would be the "spiritually mature" thing to say. But in reality I believed with all my heart that *this* was our time. I think I would have literally exploded if I had any more expectation coursing through my body.

It was difficult to worship because I was so distracted. All I cared about was seeing the man with the snow-white hair and beard walk out on the stage to begin to call out words of knowledge, which would certainly include a word for a man born with a deformity in his left arm. I was poised like a runner waiting for the starting gun to fire. The first session passed without a call for us to come forward. I calmed down a little and tried to follow the schedule of workshops and meals. On the surface I actively participated, but all I really cared about was getting to the next main session with John Wimber.

It was now the last session, and we would be boarding a plane to St. Louis the next morning. I found myself a bit irritated that Mark wasn't as anxious as I was about our last opportunity for a miracle. Finally, when I couldn't stand another second of anticipation, I boldly announced to my husband and our friends that I was going to walk up to John and ask him to pray for Mark. I could see the hesitancy in everyone's eyes, but I had not come this far to sit in my seat and passively allow our destiny to go unfulfilled. It was our last chance. I was trembling but determined to be bold. I had to convince the gentle giant to pray for my husband. I walked all the way to the front where Mr. Wimber was sitting and touched him on the shoulder. I suddenly felt my boldness melt into panic, but I had come this far and was not going to turn back now.

"Will you please pray for my husband? We've come all the way from St. Louis, and we go to Randy Clark's church. We have had many words of knowledge that God was going to create an arm and a hand for him, and I know God led us here because you're supposed to pray for him." I will never forget his response to me: "God hasn't spoken to me about that." Now, I knew from the teaching I had received that Jesus did only what He saw the Father doing, and that John used the same guideline in his ministry. But could John really be refusing to pray for Mark? Hadn't God set this whole thing up? How could John be turning me away? I'm sure he saw my heart break. I asked one more time, "Can't you pray?" I don't remember his exact words at that point, but the answer was a gentle but certain no.

I'm not sure how my shaky legs carried me back to my seat, but I got there. I don't think I've ever cried so hard in public. Mark tried to comfort me, but I was shattered and couldn't hear anything until Mr. Wimber got up to preach. It felt as if everything and everyone in the room disappeared as his words poured over my heart. John's first words were, "Sometimes the party isn't for you." He then described a child's birthday party with balloons, cake, friends, and gifts all for this one special little person on his special day. During the party the child's little brother sat alone on the sideline feeling confused and overlooked. Then I got it. This was not my birthday. My birthday was coming, and I would have a party then. It just wasn't today. Feeling grieved, we went back to the home where we were staying. We didn't talk much, but Mark did say these words: "Tammy, all I know is that we were obedient to come to the conference." To this day we both feel confident that going to Anaheim was an act of obedience.

Regaining Hope

So what do we do to regain hope when we've experienced disappointment? The beginning of Romans 5 assures us that hope will not disappoint us.

> Therefore, since we have been justified through faith, we have peace with God through our Lord Jesus Christ, through whom we have gained access by faith into this grace in which we now stand. And we rejoice in the hope of the glory of God. Not only so, but we also rejoice in our sufferings, because we know that suffering produces perseverance; perseverance, character; and character, hope. And hope does not put us to shame, because God's love has been poured out into our hearts through the Holy Spirit, who has been given to us.
> —Romans 5:1–5

This passage takes us through a progression of how we recapture hope—a hope that does not disappoint us. This progression starts with the disappointment we've encountered or the pain we have suffered. The church has many ways of looking at suffering. How we respond to suffering has much to do with how we view it. Is suffering from God or isn't it? One camp within the church believes that *God allows all suffering*, and they embrace it as an opportunity to share in the sufferings of Christ. This camp emphasizes verses that talk about taking up your cross (Mark 8:34), rejoicing in your suffering (Rom. 5:3), and expecting trials (James 1:2–4).

If not careful, though, they could subtly begin to rejoice in the suffering rather than in the process that leads out of suffering. Romans 5 says, "We also rejoice in our suffering" (v. 3) but then it goes on to explain why: "because we know that suffering *produces* perseverance; perseverance, character; and character, hope" (vv. 3–4). It is important to *produce through* the suffering rather than *valuing being in* the suffering.

Others in the church believe that *suffering does not have its source in God*, but that it is from the enemy. They fight against the devil so their suffering will end. This camp emphasizes verses about God providing for all our needs (Phil. 4:19), about our approaching the throne of grace with confidence to make our requests to God (Heb. 4:16), and about being qualified to share in Christ's inheritance (Col. 1:12). Again in Romans 5 it says, "We also rejoice in our sufferings," but then speaks of a *process* of regaining hope rather than an instantaneous way out of the suffering. It is vital to embrace the process when God doesn't provide immediate relief.

If both camps support their beliefs with Scripture, then which one should we turn to in our suffering? We believe there is a time for each. Suffering leads to perseverance, but to have the strength to persevere we must learn to be at peace and to rest in God at some times and at other times to be at war and fight the lies of the enemy. One of the results of disappointment is learning when to rest and when to fight. Ultimately, if we allow it to, disappointment can lead us into a deeper intimacy with our Father.

The Bible says there is a time for everything:

> There is a time for everything, and a season for every activity under the heavens: a time to be born and a time to die, a time to plant and a time to uproot, a time to kill and a time to heal, a time to tear down and a time to build, a time to weep and a time to laugh, a time to mourn and a time to dance, a time to scatter stones and a time to gather them, a time to embrace and a time to refrain from embracing, a time to search and a time to give up, a time to keep and a time to throw away, a time to tear and a time to mend, a time to be silent and a time to speak, a time to love and a time to hate, a time for war and a time for peace.
>
> —ECCLESIASTES 3:1–8

One of the most powerful and helpful books we have ever read is *The Fire of Delayed Answers* by Bob Sorge. Bob was the worship leader of a large church when his vocal chords became damaged to the point that he could no longer sing. That happened twenty years ago, and he still trusts that God will heal him. He says:

> God wants you to become fully surrendered to the fullness of His will and purpose for your life (quietness), and He also wants to heal you (confidence). The two seem almost contradictory at times, so let me express as clearly as I can my best understanding of God's ways in this arena: It's God's will to heal you, to provide your financial needs, and to answer all your prayers, that are according to His will, but sometimes He delays the answer in order to work a greater surrender in our hearts.[1]

There is a time to rest in quietness and a time to fight with confidence, but how do we know what it's time for now? We know by asking God and listening for His direction.

DISCERNING WHETHER TO REST OR FIGHT

Over the twenty years that we've been waiting for our miracle, Mark and I have had seasons of pressing in for our promise when we've battled to take our thoughts captive and have renounced the lies of the enemy. We've also had times of being still before our Father, laying our burdens at the cross and resting in the Spirit. Sometimes, we have been in rest mode and then God catapulted us into fight mode. Other times we have been in fight mode and God has called a halt and drawn us into rest mode. By nature,

Mark and I are more comfortable resting. We both tend to be peacemakers. We gravitate toward mercy over justice and stillness over battle. However, we have learned not to assume that God will call us only to rest. As with all believers, God sometimes calls us to fight. Here are some of the ways we've experienced God's guidance in showing us whether to rest or to fight.

Through scripture

God will highlight scripture as we spend consistent time in His Word. Certain passages will leap off the page and come to life. The verses resonate in our hearts and excite our spirits, and we know that God is speaking, calling us to something new.

I recently resigned my position as a full-time teacher. Mark and I felt that it was time for me to work part-time as a substitute teacher so I could have time to focus on this book, which we view as part of living our promised miracle. That meant a drastic reduction in salary. At the same time, our only child, Angela, was planning her wedding. Mark had been praying intensely for provision to pay off college loans, finance the wedding, and pay for our daily expenses. He never doubted God's promise to provide, but he also felt compelled to pray according to the scripture that says, "If any of you lacks wisdom he should ask God" (James 1:5). Angela was creating bookmarks with Bible verses as favors to hand out at her wedding reception. One of the passages she chose to use was Matthew 6:25–27:

> Therefore I tell you, do not worry about your life…Look at the birds of the air, they do not sow

or reap or store away in barns, and yet your heavenly Father feeds them. Are you not much more
valuable than they? Can any one of you by wor-
rying add a single hour to your life?

Now Mark had read this verse hundreds of times, but
this time God highlighted something unexpected. The
words that leapt off the page were: "Therefore, *I* tell you..."
Mark knew in his spirit that God was saying: "Hey, don't
just race past this because it is so familiar to you. I, your
heavenly Father, am telling you, Mark, not to worry. This
verse is for you right now. I've got this thing covered. Just
let yourself rest."

Over the next several days God highlighted similar
verses about resting as confirmation to Mark that he was
not mistaken in what he was feeling led to do. It's amazing
how God can drive a point home when He wants to make
sure we get it.

Through grace

God may switch you from fighting to resting or from
resting to fighting by giving or taking away grace. If you
are exhausted and depleted from the fight, God may show
you that it's time to rest. If you have been resting but feel
all stirred up and ready for action, God may show you that
it's time to fight.

One word of caution: feelings alone are not a reliable
gauge for discerning God's direction. However, if after
persevering we still feel drained from the fight or unset-
tled in the rest, then God is probably leading us to do the
opposite of what we're doing. One of the most amazing

truths about God is that He empowers us to persevere in what He is calling us to do. It may still feel like hard work, but it's satisfying. Even in the midst of disappointment we can have peace in knowing that we are in the center of God's will.

Through dreams

Another experience that is common to us is hearing from God through dreams. We have found that we are often so much in our own thoughts during waking hours that God has better access to our minds while we are sleeping.

One time Mark was asking God if he should fast for our church because he had a strong sense that the enemy was wreaking havoc among many of our members. That night he had a dream where a demonic spirit was coming after him. In the dream Mark commanded the spirit to leave, and it instantly left. When Mark woke up, he sensed the Holy Spirit saying, "Now you have your confirmation." That dream and those words gave Mark assurance that he was not getting into a fight that God hadn't called him into. He went on to fast and had the grace to do it because God had called him to fight.

After twenty-three days we received a phone call from two prophetically gifted ministers we deeply respect. Even though Mark had never spoken to anyone regarding his fast, one of the ministers told us that God gave Mark what he was fasting for on day twenty-one! The other minister then suggested that Mark may not need to continue the fast and that to do so could lead to self-effort and walking in the flesh rather than in the power of the Holy Spirit. After prayer, Mark felt released by God from fighting. He entered into a time of rest (and a time of eating).

There are other tools God uses to guide us in knowing whether it's time to fight or rest, but scripture, grace, and prophetic dreams are the three most common ways He speaks to us.

THE BENEFITS OF DISAPPOINTMENT

Disappointment is hard, but it can build godly character in us. A child given everything on demand can become arrogant, ungrateful, disrespectful, and selfish. On the other hand, a child who learns to wait and persevere is often humble, grateful, respectful, and compassionate. The bottom line, like it or not, is that it is good for us to have to persevere sometimes.

Perseverance produces character.

The Bible gives us example after example of people who waited to see the fulfillment of promises God made to them. Abraham waited twenty-five years for Isaac to be born. Moses led the Israelites through the desert for forty years before they entered the Promised Land. David was anointed to be king as a youth yet he didn't have access to the throne until years later. Mary the mother of Jesus waited more than thirty years to see her Son fulfill His destiny as the Messiah. All of these persevered through disappointment and all grew in character.

There is no doubt that persevering through obstacles

allows us to develop patience. When we are disappointed we can either learn patience or spend our days frustrated and angry. I think it's interesting that the love chapter in 1 Corinthians 13 starts with, "Love is patient." Patience is also a fruit of the Spirit listed in Galatians 5:22.

Mark had an interesting revelation from God regarding patience. The Holy Spirit brought to his mind the times he had heard it said that we should not pray for patience because we are asking for trials and pain if we do. Often following is a statement similar to "be careful what you ask for." Although usually spoken in jest, it is a sad commentary when we avoid praying for one of the fruit of the Spirit. We pray for love and joy and peace without hesitation. Perhaps we should pray for patience as well.

Adel Bestavros said this about patience:

> Patience with others is Love.
> Patience with self is Hope.
> Patience with God is Faith.[2]

Perhaps if we pray for patience with others, ourselves, and God, we'll get a dose of faith, hope, and love to go with it. Sounds like a good package deal to me.

Character produces hope.

Romans 5 says character produces hope. This one was hard for me to figure out. I could easily understand how suffering leads to perseverance. When we can't make things change, we must hang in there and trust God. And it makes sense that perseverance produces character. But how does character produce hope? How does something about me produce hope in me? God reminded me of a time when He lovingly convicted me of three things that were lacking in my character. I was crying out to Him about why Mark and I were not in full-time ministry again and His answer was not what I wanted to hear.

I've found that one way you can know you are hearing the voice of God is that you feel amazingly loved and empowered right in the middle of a rebuke. I took the next year or so to intentionally work on the areas He showed me. I took better care of my body, I prayed for my husband consistently, and I didn't assume something was God's will just because I wanted it to be. As I think back on that time I remember how I became less despairing and more hopeful by allowing God to shape my character. I was more Christlike, and that gave me hope. It wasn't hope in my ability to make needed changes in my life. It was hope in my ability to obey the voice of God through the help of the Holy Spirit. Character had produced hope in me.

Is Disappointment a Sin?

Disappointment is an emotion, and emotions are neither right nor wrong. However, disappointment that is stuffed down and left to fester can tempt us to sin. Disappointment, if unresolved, can lead us to doubt God. Make no mistake about it: the enemy has no moral dilemma over lying to us as we walk through the process of regaining hope. While we are suffering, the enemy will tell us that God is not for us but against us so that we will be disappointed in Him. We may feel as if God isn't hearing our prayers or that He is playing with our emotions just to test us. This can produce fear because we feel unprotected and manipulated. Just as I felt that God hadn't kept His promise when we didn't receive our miracle at the healing conference, you may feel that God hasn't kept His promise to you.

Here is what the progression into doubt can look like:

I don't understand, but You are *good* and I *do* trust You to take care of me.

You don't understand *me*, but You are *good* and I *can* trust You to take care of me.

You don't understand, You're *usually good*, but it's *hard* to trust You to take care of me.

You don't care, You're not good, and I won't trust You. I'll take care of myself.

If we are aware of how doubt can take root in our hearts, we can dig it out before it has a chance to grow. In his teaching "Tools for Healing Past Disappointments" Bill Johnson makes this statement: "I believe that one of the greatest conflicts to the flow of miracles in an individual life is unresolved pain in the heart from disappointment."[3]

Bill goes on to describe how he handles disappointment. He says he gets alone with God and attempts to get "gut-level honest with no religious pretense."[4] He may tell God that he feels betrayed or that God didn't back him up. The next thing he says to do is vitally important:

> But here's the deal: you do not have the right to walk into the throne room, dump your garbage and then leave. If you're going to engage in that kind of encounter with the Lord: bring it, be honest and dump it, but stand there and wait for the Lord to respond.[5]

Prayer is two-way communication. We should not initiate a conversation with God unless we have the time to listen for His response. Give Him a chance to comfort you. It is possible to be at peace and uncertain at the same time.

While persevering through disappointment, the enemy will try to convince us that we are alone, leading us to feel disappointed in others. He will bring the accusation that no one is hanging in there with us for the long haul; that they're too busy with their own lives. Feeling uncared for leads to self-pity, which deepens our sense of loneliness.

The enemy also attempts to make us feel disappointed in ourselves. He reminds us of past sin—sin that was paid for by the blood of Jesus. If we believe we are too weak to maintain permanent change, we won't be open to the work of the Holy Spirit in our lives. We give power to the enemy when we believe his lies.

Whether we are disappointed with God, with others, or with ourselves, we need to take our feelings to God in prayer so that He can bring resolution. This may surprise you, but there was a time when I felt that prayer didn't help me feel better at all. Then I came to recognize that I spent the whole time in prayer rehashing what made me feel horrible in the first place. I walked away from prayer more under the pile than when I started. Then I learned from Bill Johnson about praying *above my circumstances*.

Instead of talking through every detail of my disappointment, which God already knows, I learned to pray the truth of God's Word over my disappointment. My prayers sound something like this: "God, I feel overwhelmed and out of my league, but I can do all things through Christ who strengthens me. God, I feel angry and hurt, but I know that You love the person who hurt me and You can pour Your love for that person into me. I don't feel forgiving, but I know that You have forgiven me of much so please empower me to forgive as I have been forgiven." When I pray *above* my circumstances, rather than *about* my circumstances, I walk away refreshed and hopeful. It renews my strength.

Often, when we feel disappointed we want to know why

things happened the way they did. God may not comfort us by telling us why. The truth is that, although we may *want* to know why things unfold the way they do, we do not always *need* to know why. A better question to ask is, "What can I learn from this?" Knowing why something happened does not change the circumstance, but knowing what we can learn gives us something to reach for and can bring about positive changes in our lives.

Disappointment will cause one of two things to happen. It will either draw us closer to God, or it will distance us from God. The choice is really ours because God does not distance Himself from us. He stays put. If there's any moving away, it's on our end.

The following illustration demonstrates how we can respond to disappointment:

Responding to Disappointment

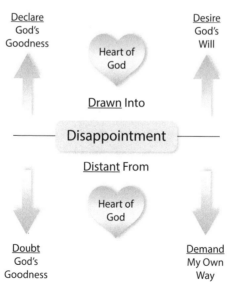

When we declare God's goodness, we draw into the heart of God because we feel safe. We can snuggle in knowing that He will shelter us and walk with us through our disappointment. However, if we doubt God's goodness, we distance ourselves from the heart of God because we feel hurt. We take a defensive stance and close ourselves off from the comfort and wisdom that only our Father can give us.

Desiring God's will also draws us into His heart, as the previous illustration shows. We trust that He is smarter than we are and that He has plans to bring us out of our disappointment. We trust that He will give us the wisdom only gained by our experiencing trial. On the other hand, if we demand our own way, we distance ourselves from the heart of God. We believe our ways are better than His and miss the opportunity to walk into something more fulfilling than we could have imagined. Pulling away from God only increases our pain and deepens our disappointment. Pressing into God may not bring the answers we want, but it does bring security and hope.

DON'T FORGET

- Regaining hope after disappointment usually involves a process of suffering leading to perseverance, perseverance leading to character, and character leading to hope.

- Sometimes God calls us to press through and fight for answers, and other times He calls us to rest and wait for answers. There are times when God's answers are instantaneous, and we neither have to press in nor wait. We can know which action to take by asking Him.

- When disappointment begins to cause us to doubt God's goodness, we must be honest with God about our feelings and then *wait for His response.* We may not get to know *why*, but we can get to know *Him*. (See Jeremiah 9:24; John 17:3.)

- Praying above our circumstances (by declaring the truth of God's Word) in addition to praying about our circumstances (sharing how we are feeling) can help us regain hope.

- Disappointment is not a sin, but it can tempt us to sin. We can either draw close to the heart of God in the midst of our disappointment, or we can distance ourselves from God. The choice is ours.

LET'S PRAY

Lord God, You are bigger than my disappointment. You are bigger than my lack of faith. Your truth is greater than the facts I'm facing. You remain faithful.

Father, here is what I commit to You: I want to follow You. I want to declare again my decision to make You Lord of my life, and I give You permission to lead. Lord, I repent and renounce not listening to Your voice because I felt too weak, fearful, and disappointed. Father, I am going to put myself out there again. I choose to give You permission to return me to the place of promise. I repent and renounce completely where I have told You I choose not to believe You anymore. Lord, You love me and with You is the safest place I can be. In Your name, amen.

When God speaks a promise over our lives, it moves us from comfort to risk and from the mundane to adventure.

Chapter 3

EMBRACING YOUR PROMISE

S HE WAS SO little and cute, only five years old, but she was not messing around when she asked this question. She was serious. It was a bit difficult for me to switch gears in the midst of counting my cherries during our Hi-Ho! Cherry-O game. "Mom," my Angela asked, "is Santa Claus real?" My mind began racing. She was still such a little girl. I believed in Santa until I was eleven, and then my world came crashing around me when I found out that my mom and dad wrote Santa's name on the gift tags. I wasn't ready to talk about this, but I had to act quickly. My little girl was quite perceptive and would take my hesitancy as an answer she did not want to hear and that I did not want to give. I had waited too long already.

"Why aren't you answering me?" she asked. Just then the most profound thought came to me. I'll turn the question back on her. "What do you think, sweetie?" With exasperation she said, "If I knew what to think I wouldn't be asking you." I had one more diversion tactic to try, "Well, in a lot of ways he is real because giving to others is…" Oh, good grief, this wasn't working at all. And then she pulled out the last straw, the statement that left me completely

41

defenseless: "Mom, *promise* that you'll tell me the truth because I really need to know." A little tear was coming, and it wasn't hers. We had long ago established a hard and fast rule in our home: if someone asks, "Do you promise?" all joking around ends and the truth must be told—the only exception is when planning surprise parties.

I had to eek out the words, "No, honey, Santa is not real." Just so that this story doesn't end on a sad note, I'll let you know that Angela and I agreed that it would be OK to pretend that Santa was real, even though we both knew he wasn't. For the next several years gift tags had Santa's name on them, and gifts were hidden until Christmas morning when they magically appeared. It was a happy solution.

Have you ever had a momentary lapse in judgment when someone asked, "Do you promise?" I have. One year, near my birthday, I was feeling rather valiant. I announced to Mark that I didn't need him to buy me a birthday gift. I knew funds were tight, and I didn't need or want anything. He was wisely suspicious. "Are you sure?" he asked. "Yes, I'm sure." And then, just to make absolutely certain he covered all his bases, he asked, "Do you promise?" Well, now that put a lump in my throat, but being the mature woman that I am, I said, "Yes, I promise." I didn't get a birthday present from Mark that year, and I had to work hard not to pout about it. Mark was convinced that I didn't want a gift. He was honoring what I told him—I had promised. It probably doesn't come as a surprise that I never said I didn't want a gift again.

A promise is a guarantee, or an assurance, that

something will happen. A promise is giving your word and speaking the truth. No wonder the Bible is so full of promises. The one true God speaks them; they are everlasting and absolutely reliable. There are promises given to all believers in Jesus: eternal life, that we will never be forsaken or left alone, and that all the weary and heavy laden who come to Him will find rest. Some promises are specific to individuals: Abraham and Sarah received the promise of a child, David received the promise of a throne, and Solomon received the promise of a temple. However, the whole world received the most wonderful promise of all: the promise of a Messiah and Savior.

After working through the disappointment of our creative miracle not happening at the Anaheim conference, we began to wonder, "Did God *promise* us an arm and a hand?" If He did promise then the deal was sealed and we had only to wait for the right time and follow any steps of obedience He might ask of us. And so a deeper level of seeking God began.

THE WORDS KEPT COMING

In September of 1993 our pastor, Randy Clark, experienced a powerful touch from God. Miraculous things started happening in our church, and as word got out Randy began receiving speaking invitations from all over the world. Because he needed help administrating all the details of travel, Randy asked Mark to travel and minister with him. Laid off from his job a month before, Mark found the invitation to be an answer to prayer. In fact, God had told

Mark that his unemployment would last thirty days, and Randy's invitation came on the thirtieth day.

Traveling with Randy put Mark in front of people he never would have met otherwise. With this new opportunity came new words of knowledge. Many of the words came from Mark to others and many came from others to Mark. Because so many people received ministry at the conferences, words often went unrecorded. We do, however, have a written account of a vision that a woman had in 1995 that was especially unique. What made this vision so powerful was that Mark was not present when it occurred. Randy made the trip to Ingram, Texas, for a conference, and Mark stayed in St. Louis to handle things at our church. She wrote out this vision and gave it to Randy. Here is what she wrote:

> I heard the Lord say: "Tell Randy Clark that I'm going to give him a hand…He's believed me for the unseen and now I'm going to show him the seen." And then I saw a hand attached to a forearm that changed in size starting as normal and decreasing to a soft little puffy baby's hand. I had a sensing that this meant perhaps that the hand was one that has been stolen in the womb.

More and more it seemed that God was building our faith and trust in Him. He wanted us to know the miracle would happen. Yet while it would seem that hearing these words from others on an ongoing basis would be encouraging, there were times when we grew weary. Time and time again we heard about God's plan to create an arm and a hand, but nothing ever happened. We didn't doubt that God kept His promises, but we did wonder if we, and others, were hearing correctly from God.

It was a difficult promise to believe, and we weren't sure we wanted to believe it. It may sound strange that we would be uncertain about receiving such a phenomenal gift, but there were so many unanswered questions. We wanted to feel normal and not so isolated. After all, there were no support groups for people who were carrying promises of creative miracles. The only way we knew to break out of this cycle of thinking was to surrender it back to God.

One night we were watching the movie *Rudy*. The movie tells the true story of Rudy Ruettiger, a young college student who dreamed of playing football for Notre Dame. His family only laughed at his ambitions, knowing that Rudy would be working in the local steel mill like the rest of the family. But Rudy's dream wouldn't die. He went to extraordinary lengths to get accepted to Notre Dame and then made it on the football team as a walk-on player, where he was treated as a human tackling dummy. He eventually won the respect of the coach who gave him *one* shot at gridiron glory. And yes, Rudy triumphed.

Even though the movie was inspirational and uplifting, it left Mark in tears. As we laid our heads on our pillows later that night, Mark turned to me and said, "Do dreams really come true?" We drifted off to sleep. I suddenly woke up hearing a cry from our daughter's room, but when I went to check on her she was fast asleep. I got back into bed and felt the Lord speaking, "You heard your child cry out to you. How much more have I heard My child's cry."

I woke Mark to tell him what I heard. All we could do was pray another prayer of surrender.

This happened on a Saturday night. In church the next morning, as worship ended, Mark tapped the shoulder of a friend in front of us to say good morning. The man turned around and his eyes got big. He shouted, "Mark Endres!" as if he was completely surprised to see us. He then told Mark that during his quiet time that morning before church God said, "If I were to talk to Mark Endres today, this is what I would say to him." The Lord instructed him to type something out. He reached into his pocket and handed Mark a piece of paper that read:

> For all [these] things are [taking place] for your sake, so that the more grace (divine favor and spiritual blessing) extends to more and more people and multiplies through the many, the more thanksgiving may increase [and redound] to the glory of God.
>
> Therefore we do not become discouraged (utterly spiritless, exhausted, and wearied out through fear). Though our outer man is [progressively] decaying and wasting away, yet our inner self is being [progressively] renewed day after day.
>
> For our light, momentary affliction (this slight distress of the passing hour) is ever more and more abundantly preparing and producing and achieving for us an everlasting weight of glory [beyond all measure, excessively surpassing all comparisons and all calculations, a vast and transcendent glory and blessedness never to cease!].

Since we consider and look not to the things
that are seen but to the things that are unseen;
for the things that are visible are temporal (brief
and fleeting), but the things that are invisible are
deathless and everlasting.

—2 Corinthians 4:15–18, amp

God had seen our tears and felt our hearts, and He
spoke through a friend who knew nothing of our promise.
The Lord's words were clear; we were to keep our focus on
what we could *not* see.

There was another time when Mark was especially burdened and weary with the weight of carrying our promise.
He was traveling a lot at the time, which meant that we
were not together much. This was difficult for both of us.
Mark had the pressure of being in front of large groups
of people he did not know as well as the stress of being
away from home. We didn't have cell phones back then,
and connecting was difficult, as we were often in different
time zones and were both very busy.

Mark had just given the announcements at a conference in Lexington, Kentucky, and had stepped backstage
to pray before ministry time began. He was emotionally
exhausted and struggling to carry the promise. As he was
praying, he felt a tap on his shoulder. A professionally
dressed woman said, "I'm sorry to interrupt, but my husband insisted that I find you." She went on to explain that
her husband was an official for the state of Kentucky (we
can't remember if he was the mayor, a senator, or a con-
gressman) and that they had left the meeting early to pick
up their child at the airport. While in the car the woman

shared an impression she had for Mark, and her husband said, "You must go back and find him."

She said, "While you were giving the announcements tonight, the Lord spoke to me to make a note and write down your name because you are one destined for a creative miracle." Mark thanked her and prayed for her. It would seem that hearing this again would only add to Mark's heaviness, but it didn't. It was as if God was saying, "I understand that it's hard, but you can't let it go." A weight lifted and Mark felt he was not alone. It was an "I am with you *always*" moment, and it touched Mark deeply. More than having an intellectual knowledge of Scripture, he truly understood the truth of God's presence with him.

God heard Mark's cry and had compassion, but He would not change His plan based on Mark's feelings.

THE INVESTMENT OF
CARRYING A PROMISE

We invest in something because we have decided it is valuable and we want to share in that value. We make every effort to pursue, guard, and secure that something. When we are carrying a promise from God, we invest on several levels.

We invest *intellectually* by renewing our minds.

Investing intellectually takes a promise from the realm of impossibility to the realm of responsibility. As we *think on* what the Bible says, we discover that all things are possible with God and that faith is confidence in what we hope for and assurance about what we do not see. No longer can we say, "This is impossible because I don't agree with it or understand it." We become responsible for believing in the impossible.

We invest *emotionally* by surrendering our hearts to God's healing power.

Investing emotionally takes a promise from the realm of impossibility to the realm of stability. As we *feel* our heavenly Father's love and acceptance, we are assured that His strength is perfected in our weakness and His perfect love casts out fear. No longer can we say, "I am too insecure to carry this promise because it is impossible." We become stable enough to embrace the impossible.

We invest *spiritually* by engaging our faith.

Investing spiritually takes a promise from the realm of impossibility to the realm of capability. As we *believe* that God has called us to something bigger than ourselves, that His ways are above our ways, and that His timing is perfect, no longer can we say, "It is too overwhelming to carry this promise because it is impossible." We become capable of trusting God for the impossible.

We must allow the Holy Spirit to teach us, heal us, and empower us in order to be able to carry our promises with responsibility, stability, and capability. However, there are strongholds that oppose the way God would have us think, feel, and believe. The Bible says:

> The weapons we fight with are not weapons of the world. On the contrary, they have divine power to demolish strongholds. We demolish arguments

and every pretension that sets itself up against the knowledge of God, and we take captive every thought to make it obedient to Christ.

—2 CORINTHIANS 10:4–5

How do our minds fight with the truth of God's Word? The most common ways Mark and I have had intellectual, emotional, and spiritual arguments with God about our promise are that we have said:

- We've never seen it before.

- We're too weak.

- Others need it more.

DEMOLISHING ARGUMENTS

We've never seen it before.

Mark has had the amazing privilege of praying for and seeing many healings take place all over the world. He has witnessed blind eyes regaining sight, deaf ears opening, and weak limbs strengthening. As he ministered alongside Randy Clark, Mark witnessed Parkinson's disease leaving a woman; he literally saw her stop shaking. After receiving prayer, a man who had four fused vertebra in his neck regained full range of motion (this is anatomically impossible!).

As wonderful as it has been to witness all these events, Mark has not seen an external missing body part grow or manifest in any way. So at times we argue (or "discuss") with God. "How can this be? It's not realistic. Others reporting these miracles must be making this stuff up." At moments such as these we have to choose to take our thoughts captive. Just because we haven't seen it doesn't mean it hasn't happened. And even if it hasn't happened that doesn't mean it can't. We must not allow what we have or have not experienced keep us from embracing what God wants to show us in the future. First Corinthians 2:9 says, "However, as it is written: 'What no eye has seen, what no ear has heard, and what no human mind has conceived' the things God has prepared for those who love him."

We are too weak.

When God speaks a promise over our lives, it moves us from comfort to risk and from the mundane to adventure. We carry a divine mandate that we are unable to produce in and of ourselves. The Lord inspires and calls us to believe for the impossible. The promise feels so big, and we feel so small. We feel inadequate in view of the revelation God is proposing for us. Mark likes to call it "eternal incompetence." We must give ourselves the freedom to feel as if we don't have a clue. In these times we are not only the deer that is panting for the Lord's presence (Ps. 42:1), but we are also the deer that intently stares into the headlights of heaven. We stare frozen at the divine offer that is before us.

While it is perfectly normal to feel this way, we must not allow those feelings to set up arguments against the knowledge of God. We can't focus on our inabilities to the point of becoming paralyzed and unwilling to obey.

Bill Johnson states:

Too many only obey what they understand, thus subjecting God to their judgments. God is not on trial; we are. A true *Cross-walk* is obeying where we have revelation in spite of the apparent contradiction in what we cannot explain.[1]

Keeping our focus on the power of Jesus is our only remedy, as the apostle Paul discovered:

But he said to me, "My grace is sufficient for you, for my power is made perfect in weakness." Therefore I will boast all the more gladly about my weaknesses, so that Christ's power may rest on me.

—2 CORINTHIANS 12:9

Others need it more.

I can't think of anything more honoring than working with children who have severe physical and mental disabilities. It has been an incredible joy for me to serve these children in the public school system for nine months out of the year for twenty years. As an outside observer you would see that I changed diapers, tube fed, wiped noses, and rocked adolescents who have the minds of infants. I was on the receiving end of more giggles, snuggles, and love than I could ever possibly give away.

The struggle that comes with this privilege is a mindset that says, "I can't desire a creative miracle for my husband because he is not critically ill or unable to care for himself." So we argue "discuss" this with God, saying. "Not us, Lord. Create the missing body part for someone who needs it more, someone who has doctor bills they can't pay, who lives with constant pain, who's younger and needs to experience life, who's older and doesn't have much time left."

Again, we must take our thoughts captive. We must remind ourselves that God's power is limitless and His resources are boundless. Our receiving a miracle doesn't use up strength God could spend on someone else. There is more than enough love and power to go around. With hearts of gratitude we must receive whatever our heavenly Father wants to give us and then use it to bless others and to glorify Him. He said, "Come, all you who are thirsty, come to the waters; and you who have no money, come, buy and eat! Come, buy wine and milk without money and without cost" (Isa. 55:1).

The Danger of Comparing

In the three ways we argued with God, we were comparing. We compared what we've seen (healing miracles) with what we haven't seen (creative miracles); we compared how we felt (weak) with how we think we should have felt (strong); and we compared our circumstances (fortunate) with the circumstances of others (less fortunate). We not only judged God as unwilling, but we also judged ourselves as incapable and others as more deserving. Comparing leads to judgment, and if our judgments are not in line with God's, we are not able to embrace our promises. When we think about comparing, we typically think of comparing ourselves with others and finding them more beautiful, more talented, and more satisfied. If we let this comparison go unchecked, it can lead to envy, which is sin.

But there is another danger in comparing and that is in judging ourselves unworthy. When we determine that we are unworthy of God's blessings, we fight against His plan to bless us, and that is also sin. It is not our place to decide how God should bless us. Giving Jesus control of our lives means letting go of sin and embracing the promises He has for us. Jesus died to bless us, and by refusing to receive His blessings, we are dishonoring His sacrifice.

We see an example of this in the Gospel of John.

> Peter turned and saw that the disciple whom Jesus loved was following them. (This was the one who had leaned back against Jesus at the supper and had said, "Lord, who is going to betray you?") When Peter saw him, he asked, "Lord, what about him?" Jesus answered, "If I want him to remain alive until I return, what is that to you? You must follow me."
>
> —JOHN 21:20–22

Peter wanted to know what Jesus planned for John. Jesus was clear to say that it was not Peter's concern. Peter needed to focus on what Jesus planned for him. Comparing ourselves with others diverts our attention from what really matters.

THE SUBTLE TRAP OF UNBELIEF

In the Book of John Jesus is confronted by anxious Jews, wanting Him to tell them once and for all if He was the Son of God.

The Jews gathered around him, saying, "How long will you keep us in suspense? If you are the Messiah, tell us plainly." Jesus answered, "I did tell you, but you do not believe. The works I do in my Father's name speak for me, but you do not believe because you are not my sheep. My sheep listen to my voice; I know them, and they follow me.

—JOHN 10:24–27

The Jews were expressing frustration to Jesus. They were demanding an answer. Their demand would probably sound something like this today: "Just stop messing around and shoot straight with us; tell us who You are!" Jesus was straightforward with His answer: "I told you (words), and you don't believe; I showed you (miracles), and you don't believe." Then Jesus told them why: "You don't believe because you are not my sheep." But Jesus didn't just leave them hanging there. He went on and described the behavior of His sheep. "My sheep listen to My voice, and My sheep follow Me." And again, Jesus told them why: "because I know them; I have a relationship with them."

When we allow Jesus to know us by letting Him into the secret places of our hearts and giving Him lordship, He assures that we:

- Will listen and hear His voice

- Will have relationship with Him

- Will follow Him

I can imagine what some of you are thinking: "But I don't always get it right." Jesus didn't say that we would always follow Him in a straight line. We may take a right, we may take a left, we may go down in the valley, or we may come up on a mountain, but He declares we will listen for His voice; we will be found, and we will follow.

Embracing our promise is about staying in relationship, listening, and following Jesus. If we make it about performance or perfection, we will fall into the subtle trap of unbelief because we will be disappointed in ourselves and unable to believe that God could want something wonderful for us.

Jesus performed miracles in the sight of the Jews, and yet many did not believe. They still said to Jesus, "How long will you keep us in suspense? If you are the Messiah, tell us plainly." Miracles and the fulfillment of promises in and of themselves do not settle our faith issues. Our assurance must come from who Jesus is—the Messiah—and who we are in Him: His sheep.

Miracles and fulfilled promises are acts of love that stem from that relationship, but they do not define the relationship. Likewise, statements such as, "Yes, Jesus raised Lazarus from the dead but He did not raise my baby;" or, "Sure, Jesus healed the woman who was bleeding but He didn't heal my mother," stem from a broken heart, but they do not define the relationship. If we have surrendered our hearts to the lordship of Jesus, we are continually His sheep, in times of joy and in times of grief. We will follow Him because He says we will.

FACT VS. TRUTH

As God encourages and pushes us toward everything He wants for us, we must recognize that there is often a difference between the *facts* of our circumstances and the *truth* of His promises. As we discussed previously, Abraham had been given a promise that he would be the father of many nations, but his body was old and so was his wife's. Yet the Bible says:

> Against all hope, Abraham in hope believed and so became the father of many nations, just as it had been said to him, "So shall your offspring be." Without weakening in his faith, he faced the *fact* that his body was as good as dead—since he was about a hundred years old—and that Sarah's womb was also dead. Yet he did not waver through unbelief regarding the promise of God, but was strengthened in his faith and gave glory to God, *being fully persuaded that God had power to do what he had promised.* This is why "it was credited to him as righteousness."
> —ROMANS 4:18–22, EMPHASIS ADDED

The *fact* was that Abraham and Sarah were unable to have a child. The *truth* was that God had the power to do what He promised: to make Abraham the father of many nations. Because God has given us—and you—a specific promise and it is precious to Him, He will take us to the place of His promise. He loves us and is not going to let it go.

When we decide to believe, we say to the Lord, "I will

follow You, Lord, because You say I will." We are not trusting in our own ability when we make that statement, we are trusting in God's ability to fill us and empower us to follow Him.

DON'T FORGET

- We must be willing to give our promise back to God. If He doesn't take it back, then we know that it is ours and He will fulfill it.

- We must demolish arguments that set themselves up against the knowledge of God and take every thought captive to the obedience of Christ (2 Cor. 10:5).

- Carrying a promise from God is an intellectual, emotional, and spiritual investment. If we surrender to God's work in us, He will make us responsible, stable, and capable.

- Comparing ourselves with others diverts our attention from what really matters. Our concern should be Jesus's plan for us.

- There is often a difference between facts and truth. We see the facts of our circumstances through natural eyes, and the facts can make miracles seem impossible. We see the truth of our circumstances through God's eyes, and with God all things are possible.

LET'S PRAY

Lord, I want to give my life to You afresh. I want to follow You. I believe that You will empower me to hear Your voice and to follow You. I believe You can protect my fellowship with You. I give You all my own strength, and I exchange it for Yours. Today, right now, I ask You to make a great exchange of faith. Place my faith in Your ability to anoint me to follow You, to continually hear Your voice, to trust You, to fellowship and walk with You, and to experience every good and perfect gift that You promised. I come and I reconnect my heart and my spirit and my mind and my emotions and ask You to be Lord. Heavenly Father, please go right around those obstacles that I have constructed. Go over them, through them, whatever You have to do. Your eyes are upon me, and Your eyes are going to and fro to strengthen those who are fully Yours. Fill me, Lord. Prepare the soil of my heart and my spirit through what You desire to do. Find faith in me because You've prayed my faith would remain. Give me the gift of faith toward You. Amen.

We should not idolize our promises, but it is completely appropriate to treasure them.

Chapter 4

TREASURING THE UNSEEN

OVER TIME MARK and I chose to believe (*trust, accept, and fully commit to*) God's promise over our lives. We believed God would create an arm and a hand for Mark. I didn't fight it anymore. We knew we had no control over when or how the miracle would happen, and God wasn't talking with us about it.

But now a new struggle began. Mark and I longed to be back in ministry, and as this desire kicked in, my patience flew out the window. At this point we had been living in Colorado for four years and had not been in full-time ministry since we moved there on June 12, 1998.

So although we believed now more than ever that the promise would be fulfilled, it was not something we prayed or even talked about. It was in the background, but the desire for ministry was front and center. I was begging God for open doors. My communication with God became pleading, and I expressed frustration over what seemed to be His lack of interest in our desperation. I'm not sure how He broke through my accusing attitude, but in His mercy He let me hear His voice. He said: "Ministry has become an idol; you want it more than you want Me."

It reminded me of Revelation 2:4, "Yet I hold this against you: You have forsaken the love you had at first."

That word stopped me cold. I felt a bit confused, but I no longer used my self-entitled tone. "But Lord, these desires came from You, and I just want to move off of dead center." I then asked the Holy Spirit to show me how to know the difference between pressing in for His will in our lives and making ministry an idol. I clearly heard these three criteria.

Ministry (or your promise) has become an idol if:

- You are angry with God because the promise hasn't come to pass yet.

- You are jealous of others who are already walking in the fulfillment of their desires.

- The only prayers you are praying are for yourself.

Sadly, I met all three of these criteria—but thankfully, I felt convicted and not condemned. I repented of wanting "it" more than I wanted Him. If we continuously ask the question, "Can I have *it* now?" the answer will be no until the time God has ordained. But we can continuously ask, "Can I have *You* now?" The answer will always be *yes*. Our desire for ministry takes its proper place. We can let go of anger, jealousy, and selfish ambition and allow God to begin the work of deeper healing.

I have found that keeping our first love when we desire to serve others can be challenging. We can ever so subtly begin to focus on serving the needs of others and lose sight of our own need to focus on His presence and loving Him. Jesus told His disciples:

> I no longer call you servants, because a servant does not know his master's business. Instead, I have called you *friends*, for everything that I learned from my Father I have made known to you.
>
> —JOHN 15:15, EMPHASIS ADDED

SLAVE OR FRIEND?

It may seem that Jesus contradicts Himself when He says in Matthew 20:26 that whoever wants to be great among you must be your *servant*, but then says in John 15:15, "I no longer call you servants because a *servant* does not know his master's business" (emphasis added).

Does Jesus want us to be servants or not? The answer lies in understanding that there are two different meanings for the word *servant* in these passages. In Matthew 20:26 the Greek word translated *servant* means "minister." Jesus is saying that to be great, you must minister to others. In John 15:15 the word translated *servant* means "slave."

It may help us to summarize it this way: Jesus says, "I no longer call you slave because a slave does not know his master's daily family business. But now I (Jesus) call you friends because I make known to you everything I have learned from the Father."

A servant/slave performs for God. A servant/friend works with God. It is the Father's desire to use us to meet one another's needs and serve Him out of a place of freedom and joy, not that we work for one another and serve Him out of a place of obligation and drudgery. Staying connected with Jesus, abiding in our first love, is vital if we are to please Him while serving others. The following illustrations note the difference:

Performing for God (servant/slave)

Working with God (servant/friend)

A TIME TO CONCEAL
AND A TIME TO REVEAL

While we should not idolize our promises, it is completely appropriate to treasure them. Luke 2:19 and 51 refer to Mary the mother of Jesus treasuring in her heart all these things the angels spoke and that Jesus did. Even though she didn't fully understand what God was doing, she treasured the promise He had birthed in her. She treasured the role she had been called to play in the kingdom of God. We have permission to treasure the same things in our lives. We can treasure having Jesus live inside of us, we can treasure the promise God is birthing in us, and we can treasure our roles in the kingdom of God.

Have you noticed that treasures are sometimes revealed and sometimes concealed? Museums display beautiful works of art, ancient artifacts, and precious gems. Some types of treasures are concealed deep within the ocean or under layers of earth. The same is true of our treasures, our promises from God, and our experiences with God. There are times when these are so precious and so personal that it is impossible to find words to display them. We tuck them safely away in our hearts and talk only with our heavenly Father about them, often with groans too deep to express (Rom. 8:26). This has been true of our promise of a hand and an arm for Mark, until the writing of this book.

Others times we open up and display or give testimony to the work that God is doing in our lives, as described in the Gospel of Matthew:

> You are the light of the world. A town built on a hill cannot be hidden. Neither do people light a lamp and put it under a bowl. Instead they put it on its stand, and it gives light to everyone in the house.
>
> —MATTHEW 5:14–15

There is a time to conceal and a time to reveal. Both glorify God.

Because Bob Sorge has gone through a similar challenge of waiting for God to fulfill a promise, we asked him to share some of his testimony. He has profound insights on the value of a promise from God and why it is such a treasure.

A PERSONAL TESTIMONY BY BOB SORGE

Years ago, in 1992, I suffered an injury to my voice. At the time I was a pastor and a worship leader, and since that time my vocal strength is very small, and it's painful for me to speak. So I have about an hour a day that I can manage and then the pain shuts me down. When this happened to me, it threw me into crisis in pretty much every department of my life. It threw me into professional crisis. What does a pastor do who can't talk? What does a worship leader do who can't sing?

I found myself in a theological crisis. I thought, "God, how can I be loving You, serving You, giving You my life, walking in obedience, walking in faith and love, and pouring my life out for the gospel, and take a hit like this? I didn't have a theology for that. I found myself in the darkest place of my life. Nobody had any answers and all I had was this: for five years or so my prayer life was basically three words: "I love You." I don't understand You, but I love You. Over and over I gave Him my love in the darkest place of my life. I discovered it's the most powerful thing you can do.

God could have left Job alone. He could have said, "Have your bickering wife; have your ten wayward children; have your safe little world; have your little bubble." But the Lord said, "Job, I love you too much to leave you to yourself. I love you too much to leave you to the smallness of what you know." If God had not interrupted Job's life and if Job had not walked through a living hell, we would never have heard of the man. But after everything that happened in his life, he stood and said, "I love You; I worship You." And we know Job's name.

In his darkest hour he was able to say, "The LORD gave, and the LORD has taken away; blessed be the name of the LORD" (Job 1:21, NKJV). Psalm 11:5 says, "The LORD tests the righteous, but the wicked…his soul hates" (NKJV). So if you're righteous, He tests you, and if you're wicked, He leaves you alone. The last thing you want is for God to leave you alone.

Now I tell the Lord: "I have got to know You; I have got to see You; I have got to have You. And I want everything You've got for me Lord. Do not leave me to myself. Interrupt my life if You have to. Test me if You have to. But come to me, visit me, reveal Yourself to me."[1]

Like Mark and Tammy Endres, I have been holding to

a promise from God for years. The Lord has promised to heal my voice, and I am fervently waiting on Him until He sends from heaven and saves me. I have not yet touched the fulfillment of His promise. I am not discouraged by this, however, but am actually encouraged. Let me explain why.

One of the most valuable things you can have in this life is a promise from God. The Bible says, "By which have been given to us exceedingly great and precious promises, that through these you may be partakers of the divine nature" (2 Pet. 1:4, NKJV). The reason promises from God are "exceedingly great and precious" is because they are guarantees that, before our story is finished, God is going to visit us with His power and glory.

When God has not yet answered, we get discouraged all too easily with the fact that we haven't yet experienced our breakthrough. What we fail to fully appreciate is the amazing treasure that we actually possess—a promise from God.

The first thing I want to say to everyone who has a promise from God is this: do everything in your power to keep your fingers wrapped around that promise! It's just too precious to lose. When holding to a promise for a long time, we're often tempted to lose heart and relinquish our hope. The reason it's so imperative to hold fervently to your promise is this: jettisoned promises can be lost forever. Not every promise is unconditional. Some promises must be carried tenaciously if we are to see their fulfillment. We see this truth in the following verses:

Do not become sluggish, but imitate those who through faith and patience inherit the promises.
—HEBREWS 6:12, NKJV

And let us not grow weary while doing good, for in due season we shall reap if we do not lose heart.
—GALATIANS 6:9, NKJV

Therefore do not cast away your confidence, which has great reward. For you have need of endurance, so that after you have done the will of God, you may receive the promise.
—HEBREWS 10:35–36, NKJV

Hold on to your promise like a wide receiver holding on to a football. As he sets his eyes on the goal line, he says within himself, "No matter what happens, I must not let go of this football!" That's how intently we must resolve to hold fast to our confidence.

I can hardly imagine anything more tragic than to receive a promise from God but then to fumble it because it wasn't fulfilled in our timing. To once have a promise, but to be now without it, is like subsisting in a wasteland of heartsick hopelessness.

My soul refuses to live in the badlands of abandoned promises. I am resolved to do whatever I must to keep His promise close to my heart. Fasting, prayer, and Word immersion are gifts from God to empower us to maintain our grip on His promise.

When you have a promise firmly in your possession, an uncommon boldness and confidence overtakes your soul.

If a promise is unfulfilled, that means it must be fulfilled in your lifetime. That confidence puts boldness in your soul about the present.

Let me explain what I mean with some biblical examples. Abraham had a promise that God would make him into a great nation (Gen. 12:2), even though his wife was barren. At a time when Abraham still had no son, Lot was taken captive by invaders. In response Abraham mobilized the entirety of his resources—318 men—against the federation of foreign armies (Gen. 14:14). The odds were stacked miserably against Abraham, but promise had placed a boldness in his spirit, and he stepped forward audaciously to engage the enemy. Guess who won? The man who carried a promise. A legion of foreign armies can't kill a man with an unfulfilled promise.

Caleb had been promised a mountain in Canaan (Josh 14:9, 12). Not only did that promise empower him to endure the forty-year trek through the wilderness, it also preserved his body so that at age eighty-five he had the strength and energy of a forty-year-old (Josh. 14:11). God preserved his strength so he could take and inhabit the promise given him forty-five years earlier.

David had been promised the throne when he was anointed as king by Samuel (1 Sam. 16:13). That promise put brash boldness into David's spirit, so much so that he went up against Goliath, a seasoned champion of the Philistine army (1 Sam. 17:48). After all, how can a man of faith who carries a powerful promise and is led by the Holy Spirit be taken out prematurely by an uncircumcised Philistine?

Jesus promised Peter that he would live to an old age (John 21:18). When he was imprisoned by Herod (Acts 12:3), he wasn't old yet. That's why, even though he was slated for execution on the following day, he lay fast asleep between his two guards. Why stay up and fret when you're living under the shelter of an unfulfilled promise? The promise that he would reach an old age gave Peter the confidence to get a solid night's sleep before his seemingly inescapable death. And, of course, we know the story—Peter was released from prison by an angel (Acts 12:11). Why? It was impossible for him to die before he was an old man.

If you have a promise from God, allow that promise to put this same kind of boldness in your soul. OK, so you haven't received your breakthrough yet. OK, so all you have is a promise. But that is an amazing gift. Do you know what a treasure you have?

DON'T FORGET

- It pleases God to call us friends. He desires that we serve from a place of freedom and love. Our focus should remain on Him so that we are strengthened to meet the needs of others.

- We must give our desires and our promises their proper place. We should always desire fellowship with God more than the fulfillment of our desires. Anything we desire more than God is an idol.

- Our promises are treasures. Sometimes revealed and sometimes concealed, the intent of our promise is to glorify God.

- We should never fail to fully appreciate the amazing treasure that we actually possess— a promise from God.

LET'S PRAY

Father, when my love for You cools, interrupt me! Stop me in my tracks and let me hear by the Holy Spirit, "Yet I hold this against you: You have forsaken the love you had at first" (Rev. 2:4). I will receive Your correction as a loving and merciful treasure. I pray that You empower me to always respond with humility, gratitude, and repentance. Thank You, Lord, for pursuing me and delighting in my fellowship with You. Truly Your banner over me is love, and Your jealousy is precious to me. I treasure You, Lord! Amen.

*It may seem that our past suffering
has little or nothing to do with how we
live out the fulfillment of our promises.
Nothing can be further from the truth.*

Chapter 5

LETTING GO OF CONTROL

"Y OU SAID YOU would never put all your eggs in one basket again. You said you would always have a plan B." These statements dropped into my mind after hearing a teaching on "inner vows" and whispering a very simple prayer: "Show me, Holy Spirit." God wanted to address something in my heart that I didn't see as a big deal. I had these tiny nagging thoughts that someday I would do something incredibly stupid and Mark would leave me or that he would get seriously ill and pass away. But those thoughts were fleeting and subtle. They flew in and then they flew out.

Mark was wonderful about affirming his unconditional love for me, and he was not prone to being ill. But I thought it was normal to be nervous about losing someone you love. Then the Lord connected my feelings to my past and gave me a revelation: my fear was rooted in a broken engagement that had blindsided me and left me devastated. The breakup happened before I had asked Jesus into my heart, so I had no resource for coping with such a loss. It was then that I made a decision to *never* put all my eggs in one basket again and to *always* have a plan B.

Little did I know, I had made an inner vow, and it was

keeping me from giving myself unreservedly to Mark. I held back emotionally, though I was unconscious of it. I was in a self-protective mode all the time. What seemed to be fleeting and trivial was actually intensely significant. One of the first steps I took toward healing was to give up those vows. The minister who had given the teaching suggested a model of how to pray:

> *Lord, forgive me for taking control away from You and trying to protect myself from being hurt. I renounce these vows I have made and trust You to protect me.*

So what exactly is an inner vow? John Loren and Paula Sandford, founders of Elijah House Ministries, define inner vows as determinations we make in the mind and in the heart to exert control over our lives in order to protect ourselves.[1]

The truth is that while we think we are controlling our circumstances, our circumstances are really controlling us. Vows do not free us, they bind us. They arise from judgments, and they often result in strife. Here's an example. Suppose your mother showed you little physical affection and used unkind words when you were a child. You judged her to be cold and harsh, vowing that when you became a parent you would always be gentle and kind. Now when situations arise that call for you to be a disciplinarian, you are unable to do so. You are bound to the vow you made to always be gentle and kind, and as a result you find yourself giving in to your child instead of being able to lead. The vow you made to be in control is now controlling you.

Although we operate in accordance with the inner vows we make, we often don't even know they're there. We just know that for some reason we can't behave the way we want to behave. That is when we ask the Holy Spirit to show us why we are struggling or hurting. Is there anyone we haven't forgiven? Are there judgments we have made that need to be broken?

ALWAYS AND NEVER

Marriage has a way of teaching us a lot about ourselves. When we were first married, Mark pointed out that I tended to use the words *always* and *never* without giving it much thought. The frequent use of those two words has helped to earn me the title "Queen of Exaggeration." While at first we had a good laugh about it, I came to realize that statements using "always" and "never" often come from judgments I had made. Those judgments, if allowed to remain, become expectations and eventually inner vows that control my behavior.

Remember the inner vows I had made: "I will *never* put all my eggs in one basket again" and "I will *always* have a plan B"? I didn't speak those thoughts out loud; they stayed hidden, even to me, until the Holy Spirit brought them to light. Now that I'm aware of my "always" and "never" tendencies, I try to catch myself and renounce those statements before they take root in my heart.

"Always" and "never" statements are often accusing in tone. Whether spoken or unspoken, they can become self-fulfilling. The following are simple examples of spoken always/never statements:

> You *never* take the trash out; why do I *always* have to do it?
>
> Well I was going to take it out today, but since I *never* take it out, I won't.
>
> See. I told you that you *never* take out the trash.

There are unspoken judgments that often accompany these spoken statements, and it's these unspoken judgments that can bind us and the other person to a behavior.

> He *never* does his fair share around the house.
>
> He has *always* been inconsiderate and that's *never* going to change.

During the first eight years of our marriage, I suffered from recurring nightmares that came three to four times a week. Mark knew that I had these bad dreams, but he didn't know how frequent they were, and I was ashamed to tell him. One night God graciously gave a word of knowledge through John Arnott, the founding pastor and president of Catch the Fire (formerly known as the Toronto Airport Christian Fellowship). John and his wife, Carol, had come to minister to our local church leadership team. He gave the following word publicly, "Someone here is suffering from recurring nightmares, and the Lord wants to minister freedom to you." A man in our group stepped forward. John then said, "We will minister to you, but I believe there's a specific person, a woman."

Although I usually didn't talk with Mark about it, I had told him that morning that I had another bad dream the night before this meeting. I felt an elbow in my side from my loving husband and knew I needed to respond to the word. John's wife, Carol, lovingly ministered to me for what seemed to be hours. The first question she asked was this: "Have you had the thought that this was *never* going to change and that you would just *always* have to live with these nightmares?" I confessed that I did have that thought. Carol then led me to ask God to forgive me for believing a lie, for believing that the situation would *never* change and would *always* be this way. Once that lie was broken, the door to my heart was open and the Lord could set me free. I was set free that night, and I am grateful to this day.

We need to avoid "always" and "never" statements because they are determinations that bind us and others, and they take control away from God. However, since God is sovereign and has all authority and power, He righteously makes life-giving "always" and "never" statements. Some of the most comforting verses in the Bible are promises made with these two words.

> Therefore go and make disciples of all nations, baptizing them in the name of the Father and of the Son and of the Holy Spirit, and teaching them to obey everything I have commanded you. And

surely I am with you *always*, to the very end of the age.

—MATTHEW 28:19–20, EMPHASIS ADDED

Then Jesus declared, "I am the bread of life. Whoever comes to me will *never* go hungry, and whoever believes in me will *never* be thirsty.

—JOHN 6:35, EMPHASIS ADDED

I give them eternal life, and they shall *never* perish; no one can snatch them out of my hand.

—JOHN 10:28, EMPHASIS ADDED

Just as God has made life-giving *always* and *never* statements, there are vows we can make that are pleasing to God. In wedding ceremonies couples vow to love, honor, and cherish each other as long as they both shall live. There are monastic orders that take vows of service and simplicity. So what is the difference between ungodly inner vows and godly vows?

- Inner vows exclude God; godly vows include God.

- Inner vows are hidden in the dark; godly vows are open and kept in the light.

- Inner vows build barriers between us and others; godly vows make us accountable to others.

- Inner vows create bondage because we depend on our own strength, which often

fails us; godly vows create commitment
because we depend on God's strength to
empower us.

No Hooks

Mark and I first learned about inner vows in 1995. At that
time we dealt with the issues God brought to our minds,
and we found freedom in many areas. We experienced
a season where there was not much happening in light
of what we had learned about emotional healing, and
we still weren't hearing anything about our promised
creative miracle. It probably would have bothered us if we
recognized the void, but we were busy with raising our
daughter, juggling two full-time careers, and maintaining
relationships in Colorado Springs and St. Louis. This
season lasted from 1998 to 2003.

It had been six years since Mark last fasted, but he felt
the Holy Spirit leading him to an extended fast. During that
time, this scripture stood out to Mark as he read his Bible:

> I will not say much more to you, for the prince
> of this world is coming. *He has no hold over me,*
> but he comes so that the world may learn that I
> love the Father and do exactly what my Father has
> commanded me.
> —JOHN 14:30–31, EMPHASIS ADDED

Jesus was telling His disciples that He would not be with
them much longer because the prince of this world (Satan)
was coming to see Him crucified. By saying Satan "has no

hold over me" Jesus indicated that He had the power to resist, but because He loved His Father and did what His Father commanded, He would not fight. He would die on the cross as His Father planned.

This passage prompted a cry in Mark's heart that has remained with us ever since. "Lord, we pray that there would be no hooks in us so that the enemy will have no hold on us." Mark had a sense that this was especially important if God was preparing us again for full-time ministry. Also, for the first time in a long time, the thought of receiving a creative miracle resurfaced. We had no idea the chain of events that this would set off, but we were about to find out.

One of the most powerful dreams Mark has ever had came to him during this time. Mark normally dreams almost every night, but during this extended fast he recalled having only one dream. In the dream Mark was visiting his parents' home, where he had lived as a child. His dad was sitting in a chair in the living room (his dad was not living at the time of the dream), and he said, "Mark, come over here."

Mark went over to him and sat down on the floor and looked up at him. His dad looked down, smiled, and said, "Mark, tell me your greatest fear." Mark responded immediately, saying, "Oh, that's easy, I can tell you my greatest fear for the last ten years—that I would miss my destiny." His dad smiled and nodded his head in a way that communicated that he understood. Then the dream ended.

When Mark awoke from the dream he thought, "Wait a minute. I'm not ready for the credits to start rolling at the end of this movie. I mean, where's the part where the loving daddy says, 'I know that and I'm bigger than your fear, and you will fulfill your destiny, and I say to you, "Run, Forest, run!"'" None of that happened in the dream, and Mark began to ask God why.

Mark came to realize that God had given him an exclusive invitation. Until now he could not have articulated his greatest fear, but he knew the dream showed a deep truth about what was in his heart. The Lord was inviting Mark to walk *with* Him. If God had given him a detailed game plan of how the promise would come to pass or how to fulfill his destiny, he would be so focused on the steps that he would leave God in the dust. Most of us would do the same thing. But God longs to be *with* us far too much to give us the answers we seek all at once.

Mark's dad represented God in his dream, and He smiled and was glad that Mark told Him his greatest fear. He did not, however, tell him how to fulfill his destiny or even that it would be fulfilled. Deep down in his heart, Mark knew that just being with his dad (God) was what he *really* wanted. Mark says it this way, "Don't get me wrong, I do want to know what happens in the end, but I want to walk life *with* my Father, and not just *for* my Father." Through that dream the Lord removed a hook that the enemy could hold on to. Mark became aware of his greatest fear and that his heavenly Father was committed to address it.

TIME FOR A TUNE-UP

Not long after this dream Mark announced to me that he would like to talk with someone about our marriage. He said, "I don't think we're in trouble; I just think we need a little tune-up." It was all part of making sure we had no hooks in us. I don't know if I was more shocked or relieved. I felt we needed a tune-up too and maybe a major repair or two. We prayed about who we should see. We weren't praying together much at that time but we both prayed alone. Mark was packing boxes in his office and a card that a friend had given him months before fell out. It was Bert's business card. Bert and his wife, Nancy, had a prayer ministry that assisted people in addressing emotional healing. They weren't "professionally" trained counselors, but they had helped a friend of Mark's and came highly recommended.

At the same time I was talking with my friend about this, and she mentioned a man and his wife. You guessed it: she recommended Bert and Nancy. It's not very often that answers come that quickly and clearly, so we didn't hesitate to set up a time to meet. We had no idea what we were signing up for, but God had every intention of honoring our desire to be emotionally whole and free. Bert and Nancy became dear friends to us. They provided practical advice and shared in many powerful experiences with the Lord.

Unknown to us, the Lord had spoken to Bert the first day we met him. He did not share this with us until about two months later. The Lord said to him, "I'm not doing a tune-up for them; it will be a complete overhaul." And then, "I am going to be giving him [Mark] an arm and a hand." God, in His kindness, made Bert aware of His promise to us before we ever felt safe enough to share it with him. This was such a blessing because Bert and Nancy didn't think we were one bit crazy. They understood the intensity of what we were facing and of what we would face in the future.

During our time of meeting with Bert and Nancy, some significant inner vows came to the surface. Mark had not traveled to minister with Randy Clark for six years, and Angela and I had never gone on an international trip with Mark. So in the summer of 2004 we boarded a plane and headed for Brazil to be part of a Power Invasion Conference with Global Awakening. It was an exciting time, and it was great to be able to pray with people and see God bring healing.

One afternoon Angela was shopping with some girls, and Mark and I were resting in our hotel room. I asked Mark, "When was the last time we got a word of knowledge about your arm?" After giving it some thought, we came to realize that it had been four years since God had spoken to us directly or through others about a creative miracle. We were surprised that so much time had passed, and we wondered why God had been so silent on the subject. And then this thought dropped into my mind: "We told God we didn't want to hear about it anymore."

I mentioned this to Mark, and we both recalled saying something like this to God: "We've had enough words of knowledge. We don't want any more. Don't keep bringing it up unless You plan to do something about it. If You aren't going to do anything for twenty years then don't talk with us until year nineteen, day 364." It nearly makes me shiver to think we felt the freedom to talk with God in such a way. We had taken control out of God's hands in order to protect ourselves, and as a result we didn't get to hear His voice on the matter.

In His kindness God didn't make us feel condemned, but the conviction was heavy. We asked God to forgive us for telling Him what to do, and we renounced the vow that said, "Don't talk to us." That very evening a woman we did not know approached us in the main session. She humbly described a vision she had during worship in which Mark had two fully developed arms. She was incredibly gracious, and the vision was extremely encouraging. The Lord had heard our confession and had moved very quickly; we were amazed.

Renouncing that vow brought about another major change in our lives. One evening, while still in Brazil, the ministry team was broken into smaller groups in order to visit local churches in the area. Mark preached at one of those churches. During ministry time we noticed that our daughter, Angela, was off by herself and she was crying. Angela doesn't cry easily, especially in public, so we were concerned. It was obviously not a happy cry. She could not identify why she was crying, and she could not stop. Then one of the women with our team, a pastor's wife, volunteered to pray with Angela.

As she started to pray she stopped and shared that she

was shown why Angela was crying. She stated, "Oh Angela, there is great warfare in the heavens, and the reason you are crying is because you have witnessed your dad pray for others and they were healed, but you wonder why your dad is not healed." Angela collapsed into the woman's arms. Angela hadn't known what she was feeling, but her Lord and Savior did! What the woman spoke was exactly what she was feeling, and as they prayed, this tremendous burden lifted.

It was only then that Mark and I realized we had never shared our promise with our only child. She had been carrying the same desire and questions we had, but she had been carrying it all alone. We apologized and explained that when she was younger we felt it would be too much for her to handle or understand. Angela was fifteen when we went to Brazil. The concealed treasure of our promise was now revealed to our daughter, and it brought our family closer together. The Lord removed another hook that the enemy had wanted to hold us to.

God continued removing the hooks the enemy had been using in our lives. One morning, while worshipping at our local church, Mark had an experience where he had a conversation with the Lord. No one else heard the conversation because it was not audible. But it had far-reaching implications in changing his thoughts. The Lord asked Mark, "Do you remember the statement from your dad when he said, 'We always need to remember that there's someone worse off than us'?" Mark replied that he remembered. The Lord then told Mark, "I need you to renounce that statement."

Mark was surprised, but before he could ask why, God continued, "Your dad's intentions were good; however this created a place in your spirit where you were never allowed to feel bad, sad, or upset for yourself." What Mark sensed after that was that God was letting him know how important it is to have permission to feel, especially when we go through a process of healing from our hurts or wounds. Mark had unknowingly set up an argument against the knowledge of God by accepting his dad's statement. He had vowed to remember that there was always someone worse off than him. By renouncing this statement, the Lord removed yet another hook of the accuser. Mark didn't feel a huge rush of emotion at that moment, but something changed deep inside him.

A DEEP
EMOTIONAL HEALING

As we began to hear from God again about our promise, Mark began to feel a variety of emotions. Mark shares the following story about how God pursued his emotional healing.

There I was in the office of my faithful friend Bert; just two grown boys sitting and chit-chatting. We were catching up and discussing how our weeks had gone. As was our habit, we took time to pray for each other before parting. What happened next was totally unexpected.

As Bert began to pray for me, I saw a scene/event playing out in my mind. My mother and father were bringing me home from the hospital right after I was born. Mom carried me wrapped in a blanket and stepped into the trailer they were temporarily living in on my grandparents' farm. I then saw them introducing me to my twin sisters, Wanda and Donna. Suddenly, in the scene, I saw both my sisters begin to cry uncontrollably. My parents were unable to comfort them. It was gut-wrenching to watch. As I watched the scene, I began to feel their grief. I fell out of the chair I was sitting in and fell to the floor in Bert's office. I cried uncontrollably and felt deep feelings of sorrow and disappointment. If I remember correctly, the words that were coming out of my mouth were, "I'm so sorry. I'm so sorry!"

The movie playing in my head stopped, and after a few minutes I gathered myself, returned to my chair, and reached for a few tissues. Bert asked me to share with him what had happened. After I described what I saw and what I was feeling, he asked me, "Did that really happen when your mom and dad brought you home?" I told him I had no idea if it did or not because my parents and my sisters never discussed it.

About six months after this experience, Tammy and I traveled from Colorado Springs to St. Louis and were visiting my mom in her home. That evening I sat down beside her on the couch, and I suddenly remembered what had happened in Bert's office six months prior. The only people who knew about what had occurred were Bert; his wife, Nancy; Tammy; and me. Sitting next to my mom I asked, "Hey, Mom, I was just curious, do you remember when you and Dad brought me home from the hospital after I was born? How did it go when the girls first met me?" Mom's answer came immediately; her eyes got big and she said, "Oh my, did those girls cry! Your father and I just couldn't calm them down."

So there I had it. My own dear mother confirmed the very thing the Lord had allowed me to see, witness, and feel. But why did I need to know about this? What I have come to believe is that the Lord was showing me where an inner vow in my spirit had begun. Somehow this event with my sisters caused my spirit to immediately self-protect and to stubbornly make the decision/vow that I would never give people reason to experience disappointment or grief because of me again. As Bert ministered to me, we broke the power of this inner vow, removing yet another hook that the devil could latch on to.

THE IRONY OF SELF-PROTECTION

In response to being born with a disability, Mark built a thick wall of self-protection without even realizing it. God revealed what was in Mark's heart:

- I will *never* have expectations (don't talk with me about the miracle until it's time).

- I will *never* feel pain (there's always someone worse off than me).

- I will *always* protect others from feeling pain because of me (I'm so sorry this hurts you).

In their "Hearts of Stone and Inner Vows" teaching, John Loren and Paula Sandford describe the defense mechanism of self-protection as putting on a stony heart. In Ezekiel 36:26 God promises, "I will give you a new heart and put a new spirit in you; I will remove from you your heart of stone and give you a heart of flesh."

The Sandfords explain it this way:

> When we put on a heart of stone, we put on a false persona, a false personality. We take on a role, but it is not the role that Christ intended when He created us. It's a false role. It takes a tremendous amount of energy to continue to live behind a false persona, to keep that role up. It takes energy that God gave us to be living, and we're using it to keep up a wall, which brings death to relationship. It keeps out what we really want, and we become very lonely.
>
> A heart of stone is a condition of the heart that keeps out God and others. It was built for that; it was built to defend us from hurt. But that's God's job, isn't it? God's job is to be our protection. It's not our job. When we take on a job that's not ours, it just ends up hurting us more because we dishonor God, and we don't have faith that He is the one that can keep us protected. As a child we often don't know that. It's an automatic hidden structure of defense. The person who has it doesn't even know it. It's a shell of hardness that keeps us from being vulnerable or seen. But we want to be known, and we want to be seen.[2]

You would think that a person who is self-protecting would be cold and distant, but this is not always the case.

Mark was engaging, warm, and upbeat almost all the time. However, his self-protecting attitude drained him without him even knowing it. It drained him because he was not being honest. It made Mark feel very uncomfortable if Angela or I were ever unhappy because he wanted to protect us as well. He tried to talk us out of what we were feeling, and he tried to solve the problem, with or without our input. With the help of the Holy Spirit and loyal friends Mark is now free from the controlling spirit that he once used to protect himself and others.

In living a promise from God we must be open to His healing touch in our lives. It may seem that our past suffering has little or nothing to do with how we live out the fulfillment of our promises. Nothing could be further from the truth. Without the healing of our wounded hearts, we cannot be everything God has intended for us to be. We live in a fallen world, and as a result we have all been hurt from time to time. Even if our pain comes from misperceptions on our part, we must be willing to let the Holy Spirit shine light on why we react to things the way we do.

DON'T FORGET

- By renouncing inner vows we give control back to God.

- We should be careful how we use the words *always* and *never*. If we are speaking judgments over people, they will be bound to the undesired behavior.

- We must ask God to forgive us if we have believed things will never change. By renouncing that statement we open the door for God to bring healing.

- There is a difference between inner vows and godly vows.

- When we renounce inner vows, God is able to remove hooks in us that the enemy can hold on to.

- Self-protection leads to a false personality that drains us of energy. We need to depend on God to protect us as we are honest about our feelings.

LET'S PRAY

Father, forgive me for the times I've taken control out of Your hands in order to protect myself. I ask that You show me the places where I have made judgments and inner vows that have built walls between me and the people You have placed in my life. Help me be honest with You and with others. I trust You to protect my heart. If things need to change, I trust You to be with me and to bring about change! I love You, Lord.

All of us face a crossroads when confronted with pain. We often respond one of two ways: we shut down or we open up. The consequences are far-reaching; one leads to despairing unbelief, and the other leads to engaging faith.

Chapter 6

ALLOWING YOURSELF TO FEEL

T HINGS WERE NOT working out as I had hoped. Getting rid of the hooks in our lives proved more challenging than I expected. Mark was now allowing himself to feel a variety of new emotions, most of which were not very pleasant. In fact, he was unleashing a lifetime of pain that he had stuffed away. In a way, it felt as if I was married to a different man. His newfound emotional freedom required a major adjustment not only on my part but also on Mark's as well. It was common for him to say, "I don't know what happened to the old Mark. I used to laugh and make other people laugh. I used to be able to see the best in situations and in people."

Going to church was like pulling teeth. Mark avoided conversation and waited for me in the car if I didn't scurry out the door quickly enough. I was making excuses for his behavior, and it was awkward. I tried to be understanding, but I didn't understand. When I asked why he didn't talk with our friends, his response was, "I have nothing to say." He was finished meeting people's needs out of "obligation," and he made that very clear. If someone else wasn't doing well, he wanted to avoid him because he wasn't going to give "pat answers" just to make others feel better. He didn't want to give an opinion. His response to inquiries about how he was doing was usually, "I don't know, and I don't have to know."

It was hard to tell whether Mark was feeling more emotions or fewer. It seemed that he was making every effort to numb himself. The negative emotions that were welling up inside of him were so unfamiliar that he didn't know how to cope. In the past he avoided pain by expressing joy that he worked up for the benefit of others. But now the pain that confronted him was too intense for him to cover up. God was turning up the heat to propel Mark out of his numb state. It was difficult for Mark to be around people because he thought they looked to him only for ministry. Mark was on the edge of something, but he had no knowledge of where God was taking him. God told the prophet Isaiah:

> I will lead the blind by ways they have not known, along unfamiliar paths I will guide them; I will turn the darkness into light before them and make the rough places smooth. These are the things I will do; I will not forsake them.
>
> —Isaiah 42:16

All of us face a crossroads when confronted with pain. We often respond one of two ways: we shut down or we open up. The consequences are far-reaching; one leads to despairing unbelief, and the other leads to engaging faith.

- We avoid relationships and make excuses when we are shutting down; we seek

relationships and embrace opportunities
when we are opening up.

- We react defensively to questions when we
  are shutting down; we respond truthfully to
  questions when we are opening up.

- We resist change and avoid responsibility
  when we are shutting down; we are
  motivated to grow and look for ways to
  serve when we are opening up.

God wants us to open ourselves up when facing the pain of unfulfilled promises, but this can be hard to do. One day Bert told Mark, "You're going to have to deal with God about your disability again at some point." The Holy Spirit had a way of imparting to Bert just what Mark needed to hear. Even though Mark had dealt with many areas of past hurts regarding his disability by repenting, renouncing, praying, forgiving, studying Scripture, reading books, and listening to sermons, he seemed to need something more.

Mark's response to Bert was sincere when he said, "You and I both know where this is headed; I'm probably going to get really angry, yell, and have it out with God. So if we're going to do this, we need to go somewhere way up in the mountains where no one will hear me because I don't want to cause my brothers and sisters in Christ to stumble when they see or hear me going off."

Mark was acknowledging that he was willing to do whatever it took to heal on the inside, but he assumed he knew how it would play out. Even if Mark had feelings that were not so "spiritual," our precious friend Bert was not going to let this go. The cabin was booked the next day and off they went with another friend deep into the mountains of Colorado to meet with God.

Bert had asked Mark to make notes of any specific thoughts that came to him during the week. Mark remembered being eighteen years old and reading this passage of Scripture:

> The LORD said to Moses, "Say to Aaron: 'For the generations to come none of your descendants who has a defect may come near to offer the food of his God. No man who has any defect may come near: no man who is blind or lame, *disfigured or deformed; no man with a crippled foot or hand*, or who is hunchbacked or dwarfed, or who has any eye defect, or who has festering or running sores or damaged testicles. No descendant of Aaron the priest who has any defect is to come near to present the offerings made to the LORD by fire. He has a defect; he must not come near to offer the food of his God. He may eat the most holy food of his God, as well as the holy food; yet because of his defect, he must not go near the curtain or approach the altar, and so desecrate my sanctuary. I am the LORD, who makes them holy.
> —LEVITICUS 21:16–23, EMPHASIS ADDED

Something twisted in Mark's gut that day when he read this, and confusion lodged itself in his spirit. Weeks later God helped Mark understand that because of the hardened hearts of the Israelites, every detail about the temple and God's presence needed to be free from visible blemish or defect. This was necessary so the nation of Israel would perceive God correctly and reverently. The Lord then encouraged Mark by reminding him that the curtain in the holy of holies tore from top to bottom when Jesus died so that *all* may enter and have access to minister before Him.

Before Mark could tell Bert about the Lord's explanation, Bert asked him, "What happened to the curtain in the temple when Jesus died?" Bert was confirming what the Lord had spoken to Mark nearly thirty years before. The men thanked God for His confirmation and the stage was set. God had reminded them of their access into the holy of holies.

The next morning after breakfast, a walk, and a game of Ping-Pong, it was time to get down to business. The men prayed, inviting the Lord to come and minister to Mark. What happened next was unexpected. Mark began to see scenes playing out in his mind like a movie. He was completely unaware of his friends and didn't hear what they were praying. In scene after scene Mark saw angels striking drums and wielding swords with scriptures engraved on them. He could see the angels in vivid detail. Then everything went silent and dark.

The sense of void was overwhelming. He saw complete nothingness and became aware that he was looking into his own heart. Mark began to cry out loud, "Oh dear Lord, there's nothing here. I feel nothing, Lord. I can't feel. I can't feel anything." Suddenly many angels came and began applying something to Mark's heart and smoothing it into place. The angels were very intentional and concentrated on their work. Then the experience came to an end.

Mark felt as though forty minutes had passed, but his friends said it had been three and a half hours since they first prayed. He can't really explain why, but from that time on Mark saw two areas of habitual sin broken and was able to resist a temptation he had struggled with for twenty-eight years.

Mark had not exploded in anger toward God the way he expected to, but through a vision God showed him the emptiness of his heart and the healing that would come. When Mark returned from his experience in the mountain cabin, a process of emotional upheaval began. He was now honestly feeling, but his feelings swung from one extreme to the other. He couldn't find a healthy balance. One moment he felt cheated of a better life because he was born with a disability, and the next moment he felt certain that God had brought all things together for good. One moment he focused on what he could not do and felt frustrated and angry, and the next moment he felt like he could do all things through Christ. Sometimes his prayers were full of faith, and at other times his prayers were full of silent accusation and confusion toward God.

It was all frightening to me. I wasn't sure which "Mark" I was going to get from moment to moment, and I certainly had no idea what to say to him. Should I listen without speaking? Should I console and pray out loud? I didn't seem to be able to help Mark navigate the peaks and valleys of his emotions. Once when I was crying out to God about it, He answered in a way that made things clearer.

God told me that Mark was grieving and that he would go through the stages of grief as if he had experienced a death. He would feel strong sometimes and very weak at other times. It had not occurred to me that Mark would need to grieve something that he had lived with his whole life, but when the Holy Spirit speaks there is peace. And so I settled in for the process, a process that was bumpier than I expected. There were times when I had to remove myself emotionally from what Mark was going through so that I could stay strong, but I didn't remove myself from praying. As difficult as it was, I knew we would come out of the refiner's fire with hearts that were full and true.

THE SPIRAL

In his article "Grief: God's Way of Healing the Heart" James R. White describes the grieving process as neither a line nor a circle but as a spiral.[1] The spiral can head up or down. You can visit a certain stage of grief more than once, but if you are healing you will not stay at that stage as long as before. The following chart shows the difference between an upward spiral and a downward spiral.[2]

Upward Spiral	Downward Spiral
Numbness/shock	Numbness/shock
Emptiness/solitude	Emptiness/isolation
Anxiety/guilt/shame	Fear/anxiety/guilt/shame
Anger/irritability	Anger/animosity
Sadness/grief	Resentment/bitterness
Acceptance	Sadness/despair

When carrying a promise from God, we may need to go through a season of grieving what seem to be missed opportunities from the delay of the fulfillment. Even when we have a promise that something will be restored, we may grieve the loss of what could have been. If only we had not gotten sick, lost our job, gone through a divorce, and so on, then we could have traveled, kept our home, enjoyed holidays as a family. We may grieve that so much time has gone by without the promised miracle or question God's goodness and timing, even though we believe God is going to do something new.

Grieving missed opportunities takes us through the same spiral as grieving the loss of a loved one through death. We can move up the spiral to a place of healing or down the spiral to a place of despair. Because knowing how to let grief take us on an upward spiral is so vital to our spiritual growth, we want to share how each of these stages manifested in our lives and how they may apply to anyone experiencing grief over an unfulfilled promise.

Numbness/shock

As months turn into years those who are grieving a delayed promise may begin to feel numb to the hope that the promise will ever come to pass. We may place the thought of fulfillment on the back burner to focus instead on the present. We thus self-protect by dialing down expectancy so that we don't feel the pain of disappointment.

Because Mark was born with a disability, he did not experience the shock that a tragic accident or sudden death would have caused. He had, however, learned to numb himself to feelings of loss and sadness. He essentially had been stuck in phase one of the grieving process for most of his life. But God had no intention of leaving him there, and he began to feel all those emotions he had spent a lifetime avoiding.

Emptiness/solitude

God used the experience in the mountain cabin in Colorado to show Mark how empty his heart was. He then had to choose whether to keep isolating himself from others or to process the situation with the men and women God brought into his life. We will be forever grateful that God called Bert and Nancy to pursue Mark and not allow him to isolate himself. I smile when I think of their determination and outright refusal to give up. Little by little Mark became honest with himself and transparent with me. Eventually he shared his feelings with trusted friends as well.

At every point along the way Mark shared solitude with God. When he felt the most frightened, he spent three to four hours a day reading his Bible. He didn't know how or what to pray, so he read and read, underlining verses that stood out to him. Mark says, "It was something I could do; it was a respite."

Those grieving a delayed promise may feel a similar emptiness. If you come to this place, you may feel like you're not making progress, but know this: *it is better to feel something than to feel nothing at all.* Feeling empty is a wake-up call to our spirits. It may be difficult to talk with others about what is in our hearts when our circumstances seem contrary to what we hope. In these times we must seek solitude with God, knowing that He truly understands. And though we may be tempted to isolate from others to avoid having to explain the emptiness we feel inside, it is important to stay connected to others, even if it's just to one person.

Anxiety/guilt/shame

As we move up the spiral, emptiness turns into anxiety. Once again our spirits are waking up. It is more difficult to hide anxiety than it is to hide emptiness. Our thoughts become consumed with doubt, which can lead to guilt or shame. We may ask ourselves: *Did I hear God correctly? Am I making this whole thing up? Should I just let this go so the people around me won't worry? But if I let it go, aren't I doubting God and giving in to fear?*

If we have isolated from others and have nothing and no one to turn to outside ourselves, anxiety can turn into fear. We may fear that everything we have believed to be true based on our faith in God's Word is not true at all. Determining that our circumstances do not align with what we are thinking, we may begin to question the validity of the Bible and doubt God's goodness and love. This is a sign that we may be moving down the spiral instead of up. To avoid reaching this point, it is vital that we intentionally engage with believers who have a firm foundation in God's Word so we can begin moving up the spiral again.

For Mark, the unexpected loss of his job in 2008 helped to propel him through his grief. While he felt a level of anxiety before, that anxiety grew and overpowered him to the point where he was experiencing panic attacks for the first time in his life. Our daughter was graduating from high school in 2008, and Mark was certain we would not be able to send her to college. We could not afford our home without his job, and he feared going into foreclosure and bankruptcy. God was with us all the while and somehow, in the midst of all the irrational thinking and panic, He was able to communicate His plan to move us back to St. Louis where we both grew up.

We made our decision and began to see miracle after miracle unfold to get us back to our hometown. Despite the terrible decline in the real estate market, our home sold quickly, and we were able to stay in it until we had made arrangements for our move. Angela received several scholarships, which enabled her to start college, and some friends offered us an empty home near St. Louis to stay in for as long as we needed. While packing for our move, we found a report that Angela had written in third grade. She wrote about how we moved to Colorado on June 12, 1998. To our surprise, we pulled out of Colorado on June 12, 2008—we had lived there for ten years to the day. We still aren't sure of all the reasons that God took us to Colorado, but we suspect that one of the main reasons was the four years of healing we spent with Bert and Nancy.

Anger/irritability

Grieving is not an exact science, and it is absolutely unique to each individual. For example, before experiencing anxiety over being born with his disability, Mark went through the stages of anger and sadness. Through the years Mark prayed to forgive anyone or anything that led to his being born without a full arm and hand. His prayer was born out of a desire to have a pure heart before God. Mark obeyed Scripture even though he didn't feel angry. He describes his prayer at that time as an intellectual endeavor.

We now know that his heart was numb and that is why he didn't feel what he was praying. But after God shook all of that numbness loose, for the first time in his life Mark *felt* angry about his disability. He was angry at God for not preventing the disability, and his faith that God could continue to be trusted began to waver. If God is sovereign and has power over the enemy, then why didn't He keep the birth defect from happening? Over and over Mark would say, "It's all a crap shoot; God can stop bad things from happening but He may not, and there is no way to know when your number is up."

Mark was angry that God didn't protect him, and he felt victimized and abandoned. It was difficult to see him so angry, and I wondered if He would ever trust God again. There was nothing that I or anyone else could say that wouldn't sound trite or judgmental. All I could do was pray that God would break through his anger.

In an attempt to get to the bottom of Mark's anger toward God, Bert had Mark make a list of things he was angry about. Without looking at what Mark had written, Bert said the first thing on Mark's list: "You know God could have prevented your birth defect. Why do you think He didn't?" Without even thinking, Mark answered with tears running down his face, "Because He knew He could trust me."

Mark began to feel worthy of God's trust as the Lord brought scripture to his mind. His anger toward God was not sin, it was an honest emotion toward the One he felt closer to and loved more deeply than anyone else he knew.

Mark thought of Job, who questioned but did not curse God as Satan predicted he would. Job grieved deeply when he lost everything he loved, but he passed the test of holding on to faith in God (Job 1:20–22). Mark also thought of Peter, who denied knowing Christ and failed to be courageous when asked about his association with Jesus. Peter's faith in Jesus did not fail but grew stronger as a result of being humbled and forgiven (Luke 22:31–32).

At a time when Mark doubted his faith in God, God confirmed His faith in Mark. Mark's anger was out, and now he could receive comfort from his heavenly Father, who looked past the emotion of His desperately hurting child and saw a son who truly believed.

When we are grieving a loss associated with unanswered prayer, it is not unusual to feel angry. We often express that anger toward family and friends, or we might turn the anger in upon ourselves. And if we will admit it, we can become angry with God. But no matter how sharp our pain may feel, exposing our inner conflict will move us toward healing and wholeness. If we refuse to deal with our anger in a healthy way, irritability can turn into animosity, which will lead us on a downward spiral.

Sadness/grief

When being angry all the time becomes too exhausting, we may settle into sadness and grief. We will likely feel cleansed now that all those angry thoughts are out in the open. This is especially true if we have not isolated ourselves and have allowed people to love and support us. Though our sadness may leave us feeling drained and weak, it is not necessarily bad if it moves us to depend more on God and others. If we allow pride to keep us from accepting the fact that we are in desperate need of unconditional love, we will become resentful and bitter.

For Mark, after anger there were tears, tears that came at the most unpredictable times, tears that came from a place of deep sorrow. Mark didn't understand what was happening and neither did I. The tears were unstoppable. Sometimes Mark felt sad, other times he felt nothing at all; either way he cried. Mark and I were both worried about this uncontrollable outpouring of sadness. Once again God used His Word to bring revelation. Mark found comfort in the story of Hannah.

> In her deep anguish Hannah prayed to the LORD, weeping bitterly. And she made a vow, saying, "LORD Almighty, if you will only look on your servant's misery and remember me, and not forget your servant but give her a son, then I will give him to the LORD for all the days of his life, and no razor will ever be used on his head." As she kept on praying to the LORD, Eli observed her mouth. Hannah was praying in her heart, and her lips were moving but her voice was not heard.

Eli thought she was drunk and said to her, "How long are you going to stay drunk? Put away your wine." "Not so, my lord," Hannah replied, "I am a woman who is deeply troubled. I have not been drinking wine or beer; I was pouring out my soul to the LORD."

—1 SAMUEL 1:10–15

The Lord did give Hannah a son. Eli, the priest, misunderstood her frequent tears, but God understood the anguish of her heart and acknowledged her faith in Him. Mark's heart was anguishing in a way that the people who loved him couldn't understand, but the Lord knew. I believe the tears Mark cried brought him to a deeper level of healing and accomplished much in the heavenlies.

In John Loren and Paula Sandford's book *God's Power to Change*, they discuss the difference between sorrow and grief:

Grief may be worked through, healed and resolved by faith, whereas sorrow may return many times. Sorrow and tears are not marks of lack of faith. Sorrow is a healthy release of loss and hurt. For many months after grief is assuaged, tears may well up, especially at holidays or when some incident triggers a cherished memory. Such sorrow is not something to be done away with or banished, as one would cast away a demon, nor is it something to be healed too quickly. It is not something bad or evil. It is something to be endured and sweetened by. It is a mark of love's knowing the pain of loss. It will pass away naturally in time, when its work is done in the heart.[3]

Sadness is a natural part of the grieving process, even if we don't always understand where our tears come from. The danger is in allowing that sadness to become despair. Hope is what makes the difference between being in the downward spiral and moving upward toward acceptance. Hope is the medicine that heals a wounded heart. Hope looks not to our own ability but to Christ's, and that is what gives us the strength to face the future. We must always remember that beneath the pain of delayed answers is the promise of God, which does not diminish through our suffering. Our promises remain and will eventually bring hope that does not disappoint.

WRESTLING WITH FEAR

Although we saw miracle after miracle from God during our move back to St. Louis, Mark began to fall deeper and deeper into fear. I was able to get a teaching job right away and, by yet another miracle, we were able to buy a home based on my salary alone. But Mark's job search was grueling and led to nothing but one closed door after another. With every disappointment he found himself more and more paralyzed. He spent day after day applying for jobs online, but he would leave the house only for church on Sunday and to run an occasional errand.

Mark was stuck in the fear/anxiety/guilt/shame stage of grieving, which put him in danger of moving in a downward spiral. My job was very demanding and left me completely drained, so I had little to offer him in terms of comfort. I found myself resentful of my role as sole breadwinner and frustrated with Mark's inability to cope with life. Bert and Nancy were all the way back in Colorado, and no one in St. Louis had a clue what we had been through.

Now I was afraid. I really saw no way out. The enemy began to whisper in my ear, "You are enabling Mark by making all the money. You need to leave him so he'll stand on his own two feet. He'll never change if you keep covering for him." It all sounds so clearly ridiculous and evil now, but somehow it seemed true to me then. I would never divorce him, but I thought maybe we needed a time of separation. When I was at my lowest point, God graciously spoke. The message given in church that Sunday was about spiritual warfare, and a very familiar verse came alive to me like never before.

> For our struggle is not against flesh and blood,
> but against the rulers, against the authorities,
> against the powers of this dark world and against
> the spiritual forces of evil in the heavenly realms.
> —EPHESIANS 6:12

I knew instantly in my heart that my struggle was not against Mark but against demonic power that was coming at Mark and overwhelming him. Through the Holy Spirit I saw how the enemy was twisting the truth and lying to me. I had a new resolve to fight—to fight for Mark and for our marriage.

I eventually told Mark how the enemy had manipulated

my thinking and emotions. I made sure to emphasize to Mark that God had revealed His truth to me and that I wasn't going anywhere. Mark's reaction surprised me. I thought he would understand, but all he heard was that I had thought about a separation. He said that he felt like he had been kicked in the stomach and couldn't believe I would even think such a thing. He was so angry that he could barely look at me or speak to me for days. Mark's reaction dashed my hope for meaningful communication at that time, but I had a resolute assurance that God would bring this to good somehow. Somewhere deep down inside Mark knew God would bring it to good as well.

Eventually it became clear that we were battling the demonic spirit of fear. Mark struggled with the fear of being unable to provide for his family, a fear planted when Mark's dad expressed the concern that Mark would not be able to make a living as a welder because he didn't have two hands. As an adult Mark was able to prove that theory wrong, but now that he was unemployed, this fear resurfaced. We battled this lie by reminding ourselves over and over that the Lord was our provider, that we could not rely on the world or a job to meet our needs. We can't explain how, but we did not miss a payment or go without anything we needed.

The next fear that manifested was surprising and unexpected. Mark had always been healthy and seldom needed to visit a doctor. He often resisted taking medication, even for headaches or muscle aches. I just chalked it up to stubbornness. But now Mark was struggling so deeply at an emotional level that he was becoming depressed and unable to function. Two dear friends encouraged him to see a doctor. They shared how a short-term use of medication helped them through some difficult times.

Mark absolutely refused to consider it. I felt he was being prideful and over-spiritualizing the situation by insisting that all he needed was for God to intervene. Normally Mark would consider the counsel of trusted friends, and he would tell others that God does use doctors to minister healing, but he was not open in the least to pursuing medical help for himself. Then one evening, while talking with a friend, the true root of his resistance was exposed. Out of Mark's mouth came the following words: "What if a doctor told my mom to take a pill to help her feel better and that one little pill, which was supposed to have no side effects, caused me to be born like this? How am I supposed to trust a pill to make me better?"

That was it; the fear came rushing out. Out of Mark's heart his mouth spoke. Now he realized he needed to overcome his fear in order to get the help he needed. Eventually his emotional symptoms led to physical problems. One day while cutting the grass he became dizzy and disoriented. When I got home from work he asked me to take him to the emergency room. At a follow-up visit Mark broke into tears. These were tears of fear.

The nurse who was working with him was a Christian and, with great compassion, she explained to Mark how antidepressants work to balance the chemicals in the brain. Mark poured out his intense fear of taking medication. The nurse listened and was able to comfort him. Mark gave in and agreed to try taking a mild medication for a short time. There was an immediate improvement. The light came back on in Mark's eyes, and he could talk without crying. He was thinking rationally and was able to hear what others had to say. We both felt hopeful again.

Then, as Mark was leveling out emotionally, he began to have pain in his right thumb and found that it was locking up making it difficult to grasp anything. He found it difficult to squeeze the shampoo bottle or tooth-paste tube and struggled to dress himself and to write. A hand specialist gave him a cortisone shot but said that eventually surgery may be required to try and loosen the tendon in his thumb. Now another fear surfaced: the fear of losing the use of his one good hand.

During this time, God impressed on Mark's heart that he needed to apply for assistance for the disabled. If taking an antidepressant wasn't humbling enough, he now had to wrap his mind around the fact that he was born with a disability and that he needed financial assistance because of it. What was God doing here? We secured the paperwork and mailed it in. Within days his application was accepted and approved. God was using our past contributions to social security to free us from financial stress, not at all how we imagined God providing. It was humbling.

All of these experiences changed how we viewed other people in their struggles. We no longer had instant answers for people in marital, emotional, physical, or financial stress. We came to understand that climbing out of a hole wasn't always about pulling yourself up by your own effort, getting over it, and moving on. We have learned compassion at a level we didn't know before. God faithfully, as our loving Father, brought things to the surface that held us captive to the lies of the enemy. We were healing.

God's Perspective on Fear

Most of us have fears that we are aware of such as a fear of spiders or a fear of heights. These fears may keep us from enjoying a camping trip or from experiencing the view from the top of the St. Louis Arch, but they are not usually life altering. We either choose to confront these fears and get free of them, or we accept them and avoid circumstances that would force us to face them.

Other fears may seem healthy on the surface, but they control us in a way that limits our peace and joy. I remember asking this question at a church meeting where we were discussing emotions that keep us from experiencing the fullness of God: "Isn't fear sometimes good? Doesn't it sometimes protect us?" I used the old reliable example of a child not touching a hot stove for fear of being burned. What I was really thinking was this: "It is good when young people don't engage in premarital sex for fear of becoming pregnant or infected with venereal disease. It is good when we avoid unhealthy relationships for fear of being hurt."

My list of self-protective fears could have gone on and on. I'll never forget the teacher's response: "God doesn't want us to be obedient because we're afraid; He wants us to be obedient because we trust Him." That answer was a game changer for me. Over time I came to understand that God doesn't use fear to protect us or to teach us; He uses love to protect us and to teach us. I learned that abiding in fear doesn't give me security; abiding in Christ gives me security.

The Bible says:

> There is no fear in love. But perfect love drives out fear, because fear has to do with punishment. The one who fears is not made perfect in love.
>
> —1 JOHN 4:18

> For God has not given us a spirit of fear, but of power and of love and of a sound mind.
>
> —2 TIMOTHY 1:7, NKJV

When there are major decisions to make, we should pay close attention to the emotion of fear. Ask yourself these types of questions: "Am I taking this job *only* because I'm *afraid* I can't make ends meet without it? Am I taking on this task *only* because I'm *afraid* of disappointing someone if I don't?" If fear is your primary motivation, your answer should be respectfully, "No."

Because we have learned that God does not motivate us through fear, we should all proactively seek confirmation rather than reactively responding to our emotions.

There are those fears that we're aware of; they obviously affect our decisions and cause us to either confront or retreat. There are other fears we carry that are so deep we are completely unaware of how they affect our lives. Mark's fear of taking medication is an example of this type of deep-seated fear. Thankfully, God in His love and commitment to our wholeness will bring these fears to the surface in the proper time and help us to overcome them. Perhaps now would be a good time to pause and ask the Lord to reveal where the sources/roots of these fears are for you.

The Bible first mentions fear in Genesis 3:10. Adam and Eve did not have fear or its affects in their hearts until they failed to trust God enough to listen to Him.

> Then the man and his wife heard the sound of the LORD God as he was walking in the garden in the cool of the day, and they hid from the LORD God among the trees of the garden. But the LORD God called to the man, "Where are you?" He answered, "I heard you in the garden, and I was *afraid* because I was naked; *so I hid.*"
>
> —GENESIS 3:8–10, EMPHASIS ADDED

Adam and Eve did not realize they were naked until they disobeyed God's command. Their first instinct was to cover up and hide. Where they had once felt completely comfortable and free, they now felt exposed, vulnerable and afraid.

Often when God uncovers fear that we didn't know we were living with we feel exposed and vulnerable just as Adam and Eve did. When God showed Mark his subconscious fears of medication, being unable to provide, and losing the use of his one good hand, Mark felt disoriented and confused. He then had a choice to make. He could hide from God and begin a downward spiral in the grieving process, or he could surrender to God and continue on the upward spiral to healing. It was Mark's willingness to be exposed that opened the door to exceedingly more than we could ask or think.

BREAKING FREE

Despite our best efforts, sometimes when grieving we find ourselves stuck in the downward spiral of fear, bitterness, and resentment. We understand that these emotions are harmful, but we don't know how to move past feeling being toyed with, ripped off, unprotected, or abandoned by God when He still hasn't fulfilled our promise. We overcome these emotions by approaching God with gut-level honesty and by renouncing any inner vows we have made to protect ourselves from painful emotions. By doing this we take ourselves off the throne and give the control back to God.

If you find yourself stuck in a downward spiral, here is an example of how you might pray:

> *Lord, I know that You haven't sinned against me because You are incapable of sinning. But I feel hurt and abandoned by You.*
>
> *I am (angry at, frustrated with, confused by, disappointed in) You for not doing what You said You would do. You are sovereign and all-powerful, and You could speak my promise into existence with one breath. I don't understand why You haven't done it yet, but I choose to trust that there is a reason, and it is for my good.*

Forgive me, Lord, for my resentment and bitterness against You and for judging You as distant and uncaring. Forgive me for judging You as a God who inflicts pain and withholds good gifts. I renounce those judgments and release You to complete the work You've begun in me. I take my rightful authority as your son/daughter and break the power of wrong judgments and inner vows. I choose to open myself up to You again.

Thank You, Jesus, for dying on the cross so that I can be free from bitterness and resentment. I trust You, Lord. Amen.

Just a note: It is helpful to pray this prayer aloud with someone you trust. By bringing our sin into the light, we expose and break the power of darkness. We bring sin into the light by confessing it to another believer. Your friend can pronounce forgiveness over you as an ambassador of Christ and release you from shame. Your friend can also help you recognize the signs of falling back into bitterness and resentment, and pray with you again before those negative emotions lodge in your spirit. By forgiving, renouncing judgments, and breaking inner vows, you can begin to move back up the grieving spiral and be on your way to healing and freedom.

FROM ACCEPTANCE
TO EXPECTANCY

The final stage of grieving is acceptance of the loss. You may be wondering whether we truly "accept" Mark's disability if we believe God is going to work a creative miracle by giving him an arm and a hand. I wondered that myself for a while, but through our personal relationships with Jesus we've added a stage to our healing process. We've added a stage called *expectancy*. We are content and expectant all at the same time.

After several years of pressing in, Mark came to accept his disability. It may have looked to others as if he got himself back to square one, he was able to be happy like he used to be. That couldn't be further from the truth. Mark's old mantra could have been, "Fake it till you make it." His new mantra is, "I don't like some of the limitations that come with my disability, but I trust God."

Our contentment is not dependent on a creative miracle, but we believe God's Word, which says:

> However, as it is written: "What no eye has seen, what no ear has heard, and what no human mind has conceived"—the things God has prepared for those who love him—these are the things God has revealed to us by his Spirit. The Spirit searches all things, even the deep things of God.
>
> —1 CORINTHIANS 2:9–10

> Now to him who is able to do immeasurably more than all we ask or imagine, according to his power that is at work within us, to him be glory in the church and in Christ Jesus throughout all generations, forever and ever! Amen.
>
> —EPHESIANS 3:20–21

People often think they're content when they're really just complacent. It is easy to have an "it is what it is and nothing's going to change it" mentality, but that's not living a life of faith. Let's go back to the story of Adam and Eve for a moment (Gen. 3:1) and look at what tempted Eve to turn her back on God. The temptation came when the serpent planted a seed of doubt in Eve by asking: "Did God really say you *cannot have*...?" Satan attempts to use the same tactic on us, but in a slightly different way. This time he asks, "Did God really say that you *can have*...? Did God really promise?"

We must not give the enemy freedom to plant seeds of doubt over what God has spoken and confirmed. We must not let go of the promise God has made to us. We remain *expectant*, trusting that God's timing is perfect and He will do what He says He will do.

Don't Forget

- When faced with pain, we have the choice to open up or to shut down. Opening up engages our faith. Shutting down can lead to despairing unbelief.

- When we experience loss, we should allow ourselves time to grieve. Grieving is a necessary part of the healing process. If we don't allow ourselves to feel pain we are not being honest with God, ourselves, or others.

- God does not motivate us by fear, so we must not make decisions out of fear of what might or might not happen.

- When God first exposes fear, our first instinct may be to cover up and hide. It is important to resist this temptation and to run to God rather than away from Him.

- When carrying a promise from God, you may need to go through a season of grieving missed opportunities.

- You can break free from fear, bitterness, and resentment by forgiving and renouncing wrong judgments and inner vows.

- It is possible to be content and expectant all at the same time. Just because you've accepted your present circumstances doesn't mean you cannot have faith for things to change for the better.

LET'S PRAY

My Father, help me to face my pain so that I can heal. Thank You for being with me every moment, for being the very air that I breathe, for being my bread when I have no appetite, for being my resting place when the night seems to swallow my hope. I don't want to run away from this. With You I can run into it and find my way through it. I know there are no shortcuts, but as long as You are with me I also know I don't have to be afraid. Give me strength to open up and trust others even though they may not know what to say. I thank You for the plans You have for me, for being my future and my hope. I love You Father. Amen.

The desire of the Lord's heart is to make every wrong right. He has a zealous commitment to do this.

Chapter 7

TRUSTING GOD'S INTENTIONS

MARK HAD INVITED our friends to come over and pray for us. I was not happy. I had been working hard all week at a job that depleted every ounce of energy I had, and now, without asking me first, Mark had made plans. What was he thinking? He wouldn't just spontaneously invite them over unless something was brewing in him.

I had previously shared a lot about what we were going through with the women, but now we were going to have this big powwow with their husbands present. Mark was rallying the troops, and he was going to lay something on the line. What in the world was he going to blurt out? Here we were with our best friends, and I felt miserable.

Finally the proclamation came: "I want you guys to hold me accountable because Tammy doesn't trust me, and I need for her to be able to trust me. She thinks I don't want to find a job and that she will have to be the sole bread-winner of our family from now on."

What? I never told Mark I didn't trust him. I don't know if our friends were taken off guard, but I certainly was. I didn't appreciate Mark expressing my feelings to everyone else when I hadn't expressed those feelings to him or given him permission to share them. In the midst of what felt like a train wreck to me, the Holy Spirit was working. The truth was that I didn't trust Mark, but I didn't realize it. I just thought I was frustrated with his apparent contentment to be at home all day doing what seemed to me to be nothing.

The floodgates opened, and I poured out all those feelings of resentment that had lodged into my spirit. I am grateful to have friends who knew how to go before the Lord on our behalf. They soaked us in prayers, hugs, and support.

With the truth now in the light, we could begin the journey of rebuilding trust in each other and, ultimately, building trust in God. After initially feeling blindsided, I almost instantly began to trust Mark more. He knew what I was feeling even when I didn't, and he cared enough about our healing to call our friends. He didn't have a solution for our job situation, but he pressed in for help. How could I not trust a man who would be so vulnerable?

And so in the midst of learning about how to hear God's voice, how to hold on to hope, how to embrace our promise, how to let go of control, and how to allow ourselves to feel, we began to learn how to *trust*.

TRUSTING GOD'S TIMING

One of the hardest things to understand about God is His timing. Learning to trust God's timing is imperative if we want to be at peace in our circumstances. There have been scores of books written throughout the centuries about the importance of waiting on God. We have already touched on the topic of timing in previous chapters, but I want to share something that Mark once wrote:

> I often picture the following conversation with God when I become anxious and insist on moving ahead of His timing. As I rush ahead of Him I hear His encouragement: "Mark, I bless your enthusiasm and your zealousness. I want to encourage that in you. Always go for it when I tell you it's time. I know you want to go and explore. I have My eye on you; I know just how far you have gone. While you're out there, don't be surprised if you say to Me, 'God, I don't know where I'm going. I came out here and now I'm not sure.' Mark, I would love to be with you and walk with you. Why are you so anxiously running down the road of My promise for you? I see how hard you're breathing from rushing around and I hear the questions in your mind, questions that you're embarrassed to ask Me. You want to ask, 'Where is the promise? I don't see any sign of it here?'
>
> Oh, make no mistake, the promise is still there, but now is the time for you and Me to just be together. There are some things I'm still putting in place. I'm ensuring that there is protection over you and your family when the promise is fulfilled. There is additional covering and resources that I know you will need, and I'm still putting those things in place. You see, that's why it's so easy for Me to be long-suffering and

patient when you accuse Me of not loving you and when you feel like I'm playing games with you. You pout and give Me the silent treatment, but I know that deep down in your heart you want Me to be Lord and that excites Me. Because of this joy set before Me, I really want the fulfillment of the promise to be an extreme blessing in your life and not in any way hurtful or destructive. I know the pace is frustrating for you at times, but I ask you again to trust Me and give Me permission to do what is best."

Another time Mark wrote out these thoughts:

Why in the world do we want to go somewhere that God did not tell us to go yet? The Lord in His goodness is saying: "You want to run ahead and see if the roses are growing in your place of promise. You wonder if My garden of promise for you looks as beautiful as you imagine. You wonder if it smells as sweet as you have dreamed. My son, right now that place is only a manure field. If you go there now you will only be discouraged. I'm still getting the soil ready, but you think you will see a full harvest when you arrive. You long to sit under the shade of a beautiful tree of promise, but I haven't raised it up yet."

In his book *Supernatural Provision* Mark Hendrickson quotes Deuteronomy 4:12—"Then the LORD spoke to you out of the fire. You heard the sound of words but saw no form; there was only a voice"—then makes this observation:

> God didn't use a form to communicate to the Israelites lest they make a form and begin to worship that form. Actually, we may not be that much different from them. We want our *form-ulas* so that we can do it ourselves. But God wisely communicated with His voice. You see, He knew this would require relationship and encounter with Him on an ongoing basis. Our tendency would be to run with the *form-ula* and principles without the encounter, like enjoying the benefits of the Kingdom without the King.[1]

Running ahead of God comes from a confidence we have in ourselves that we are ready for the next step. The confidence arises from the fact that we've done our homework; we've prepared. We think that if we have accomplished A, B, and C then it should logically follow that D, E, and F will occur. And besides, our time here on earth is limited, and we need to get moving. It has become increasingly obvious in the twenty years we have been waiting for our promise that God does not buy in to our formulas. In fact, if we are of the opinion that we've accomplished anything apart from Him, then we have proven that we are not ready for the next step. We are setting ourselves up for disappointment or, even worse, for failure that could hurt the ones we love. We must trust His timing.

TRUSTING THROUGH HIDDENNESS

In our humanness Mark and I go through seasons of wanting God to talk with us about our promise and then not wanting God to talk with us about our promise. If God weren't so totally God, our prayers could give Him whiplash. If God weren't perfectly wise, I'm sure He'd find our prayers quite confusing:

- "Talk to us about Your promise; we're losing faith."

- "Don't talk to us about Your promise; it's frustrating when nothing is happening."

- "Why aren't You talking to us? Have You changed Your mind?"

The Lord hasn't always complied with our demands, and we have gone through times when we cried out to hear His voice only to be met with silence or with answers that had nothing to do with our requests. When we first experienced these seasons, we felt abandoned by God and frightened that we had somehow offended Him to the point of no return, thus the silence.

Later, we were introduced to a teaching by Graham Cooke called "Hiddenness and Manifestation." During times of *manifestation* we feel God's presence in our lives in intimate and immediate ways. We know in these times He's with us, and this makes our relationship with Him easy. During times of *hiddenness* we don't feel His presence, though He is still very much there. We must believe (trust fully) that we have relationship with God, even though our emotions feel numb or indifferent.

God takes us through times of hiddenness so that we learn to believe by faith and to rely on the promises God has made to us in the Bible. During times of hiddenness, we learn to walk by the Spirit. By learning the discipline of walking by faith, we prevent the enemy from touching our lives. Regardless of our emotions, we believe and are constantly assured by the truth of God's Word that He is with us and is committed to fulfilling every promise He has made.

Cooke says it this way:

> I believe that it is hiddenness which establishes our capacity to rest in the Lord. Hiddenness promotes a "quietness of soul." Our mind and emotions stilled before God. We have to learn how to submit our emotions to the discipline of life in the Spirit.
>
> To be able to bring yourself to a place of peace is an important discipline to have. Although it takes some time to learn, it is possible to develop it to the extent that you can bring yourself to a place of peace within a few seconds, regardless of the circumstances affecting you. It's just a discipline. It's no different from learning to drive a car or use a washing machine.[2]

We have come to a place of peace over His promise, trusting God's intentions even in seasons when He is hiding from us emotionally. We no longer feel toyed with or abandoned when we don't hear God's voice loud and clear every time we pray. We have learned to declare and thank Him for His presence and for His listening ear even during these times.

How can you develop the discipline of bringing yourself to a place of peace, even when God is hiding from you emotionally and you can't "feel" His presence? We suggest that you present the following three steps to God through prayer.

- Recognize your feelings.
- Realize your need.
- Rejoice in your God.

Recognize your feelings.

While it is true that discipline often involves making right choices despite what we feel, we must not deny our feelings. Deciding that we don't want to bother God with our concerns is not discipline. It is not relationship. By being honest about our emotions, even when we don't feel God's presence, we show that we trust Him and express faith with our spirits. We exercise this discipline by taking our focus off ourselves and focusing on the One who can meet our need.

Realize your need.

Acknowledging our need is necessary for coming to a place of peace. It requires swallowing our pride, stopping our strife, and agreeing that we are not strong enough to walk by faith without Him. This is especially important when we are in a place of hiddenness. We exercise discipline by telling God how much we love Him, want Him, and need Him. We choose to believe, based on the authority of His Word, that He hears our cry.

Rejoice in your God.

When we are not experiencing the manifest presence of God because we are in a time of hiddenness, we rejoice in who we know Him to be. It is helpful to pray what the Bible says about Him. For instance, we can pray, "God, You love me, and Your mercies endure forever." It is also vitally important to draw into our personal histories with God. When we are not feeling God's presence in a tangible way, it takes discipline to focus on what He has done for us in the past. Be specific, praying for example, "Lord, I remember when the bag of groceries showed up on our front porch." Or, "Lord, I'll never forget how You healed my sister." By doing this we can come to a place of rest and peace, and all we did was rejoice in who God is!

In the Book of Psalms David models the discipline of moving through these three steps and coming to a place of peace within moments. Let's look at an example:

> How long, Lord? Will you forget me forever?
>> How long will you hide your face from me?
> How long must I wrestle with my thoughts
>> And day after day have sorrow in my heart?
> How long will my enemy triumph over me?
>
> Look on me and answer, Lord my God.
>> Give light to my eyes, or I will sleep in death;

and my enemy will say, "I have overcome him,"
and my foes will rejoice when I fall.

But I trust in your unfailing love;
my heart rejoices in your salvation.
I will sing the LORD's praise,
for he has been good to me.

—PSALM 13:1–6

Although David carried the promise of being king one day, God hid Himself from David emotionally in order to teach him to walk by faith. Note how David moves from *recognizing* his feelings in verses 1 and 2, to *realizing* his need in verses 3 and 4, to *rejoicing* in his God in verses 5 and 6. And he does all this within moments!

God sometimes hides Himself from us as we carry our promises, but it is comforting to know that God is not punishing us. He is preparing us and strengthening us, both for the wait and for the fulfillment. Be encouraged that you too can quickly come into a place of peace and rest if you discipline yourself as David did.

TRUSTING THROUGH BROKENNESS

While *hiddenness* makes us feel numb and leaves us wondering why God is being so silent, *brokenness* is painful and leaves us wondering why God is allowing all that is happening. When Mark was suffering emotionally, the Lord let him know he was in a season of being broken. At this very time, a dear friend called us and shared the following dream.

> I saw a large white projection screen. Suddenly swirl patterns appeared and began to form words. The words that appeared were, "May the Lord, the God of your fathers, increase you a thousand times and bless you as He has promised!" Next the word "Deuteronomy" appeared. It also then changed shape and formed the words "Do You Trust In Me?" I then saw the Lord laughing with joy and He said to me, "Tell Mark Endres this is for him."
>
> Then the scene changed. I saw Mark on his knees in his own "Daniel's den." His body was completely on fire with holy power; flames were coming off of him. Mark was crying and praying, and a large angel was with him. I felt that this represented Mark praying through to complete surrender.

This precious, timely word from God was a lifeline for Mark. Prior to this dream he had completely withdrawn himself from praying for others. He had isolated himself from something that brought him great joy because he was afraid of being hypocritical. How could he ask God to heal others when he doubted God's intentions to heal him? How could he trust that God was hearing his prayers for someone else when he felt offended that God wasn't hearing his prayers for us? How could he pray in the power of the Holy Spirit when he felt confused in his own emotions regarding God's faithfulness?

Mark shared these concerns and this dream with our friend Bert. He simply said, "Mark, I give you permission to pray for others while you and the Father are dealing with one another." Mark says this, "It may seem silly, but that completely freed me up to continue to love others by praying for them in the midst of my own personal heart healing times with God." The Lord used brokenness to bring Mark's confidence in his own abilities to death, and to resurrect a stronger faith in God's ability to heal and restore. With Mark having nothing in and of his own to give, God could flow through him more strongly than ever.

The scriptures that motivated Mark during this time were:

> My sacrifice, O God, is a broken spirit; a broken
> and contrite heart you, God, will not despise.
> —PSALM 51:17

> For what we preach is not ourselves, but Jesus
> Christ as Lord, and ourselves as your servants
> for Jesus' sake.... But we have this treasure in jars
> of clay to show that this all-surpassing power is
> from God and not from us.
> —2 CORINTHIANS 4:5–7

> But he said to me, "My grace is sufficient for
> you, for my power is made perfect in weakness."
> Therefore I will boast all the more gladly about
> my weaknesses, so that Christ's power may rest
> on me.
> —2 CORINTHIANS 12:9

When you are in a season of brokenness you will feel completely at the end of yourself. Everything will feel shaky and unstable. It will seem that you are losing everything you once felt sure about.

In his book *The Fire of Delayed Answers* Bob Sorge explains it this way:

> Until our faith is broken, we think it's pure—especially because of the great victories we've seen. But the Lord knows how to break every natural prop upon which our faith tends to lean...
>
> In the place of brokenness, God will teach you what true faith is all about. It's incredibly challenging, when you feel totally empty, to have faith in God. But God wants us to see that our faith should not waver, whether we feel good in ourselves or whether we feel completely undone.
>
> A faith that springs from brokenness smells different. It looks different. It sounds different. It is different...Broken faith does not focus on getting people to respond because its confidence is truly in God alone. Broken faith has been tempered in the furnace, and it has a fortitude to endure great resistance. It is quieter, more durable and more fruitful.[3]

Jesus experienced the most intense brokenness that a human could endure. The words He spoke during His time in the garden of Gethsemane can show us how to rightly process our own brokenness. Jesus knew His time to go to the cross had come. He shared the Passover supper with His disciples, and then He took them to the garden.

After telling the disciples, "Stay here and keep watch," He spoke these words: "My soul is overwhelmed with sorrow to the point of death" (Mark 14:34). Jesus was acquainted with sorrow and pain. He did not repress these feelings and neither should we.

Next Jesus said, "Abba, Father, everything is possible for You. Take this cup from Me" (Mark 14:36). When we are enduring a time of brokenness, we want the pain to end; we want it taken away from us. It is not sin to want suffering to stop, but the next words spoken by Jesus are vitally important: "Yet not what I will, but what You will."

Our Father not only breaks us to bring us to the end of ourselves, He also allows the breaking in us to bring forth new life—life empowered by His resources rather than our own. Just as Jesus rose from the dead, we also rise from the death that brokenness brings. We are resurrected to a life of total reliance on Him.

TRUSTING WITHOUT OFFENSE

We have learned much about how our faith pleases God even when we feel we are not doing much for His kingdom, or when we feel our prayers are not bearing fruit. Mark learned this most profoundly as he prayed for his mother. Mark tells the story.

> My mom had been confined to her bed for fif-teen months and she needed to be repositioned to avoid bed sores. Her knees were drawn up and her eighty-eight-pound body was twisted from

arthritis. She was unable to speak or respond. Because she had so many needs, I chose to focus on one thing. Every time I went to visit, I prayed for the finger on her left hand to unlock and straighten. Time and time again I prayed, but I saw no results. The thoughts that flooded my mind became overwhelming and intense. They went something like this: "Here I am calling myself a Christian. The God of the universe has chosen to dwell in me by the power of the Holy Spirit and yet I can't even get this one finger to move and straighten up. If I really carry God's love and power then things should change."

I felt like a line was being drawn in my spirit. I feared that my response to these thoughts and emotions would determine how I approached God and others in the future.

As I was sitting next to my mom's bed being bombarded by these thoughts, the Lord began to speak to my spirit. God reminded me of a woman I prayed for in Russia in 1996. The woman was carried to me by two other women. She was experiencing kidney failure and looked much older than she was. I prayed for her, but there was no apparent change. One year later when I was back in Moscow, a beautiful and bright woman ran up to me waving a note written in Russian. A translator read the note to me, and I discovered that this woman was the one I prayed for the previous year.

The note said that three weeks after I had prayed she was completely and miraculously healed. Not only was she healed, but when she prayed for others to be healed they almost always were. Then the Lord spoke words into my heart that I will never forget. He said, "Mark, I am still the Messiah who heals the woman in Russia, and raises people from their deathbeds, but your mother is not going to get up. But blessed are you Mark, for you are not offended at Me."

To my surprise, the Lord went to a place in my heart that I didn't even know existed. There was a place within me that thought I must be offended at God. I must be offended because my prayers for Mom were not being answered. I must be offended because He healed a stranger in Russia but not my mom. My loving heavenly Father who knows the true condition of my heart—this great God—told me I was *not* offended.

First John says, "This is how we know that we belong to the truth and how we set our hearts at rest in his presence: If our hearts condemn us, we know that God is greater than our hearts, and he knows everything" (1 John 3:19–20). And in the Gospel of Luke, we read: "Jesus answered and said to them 'Go and tell John the things you have seen and heard: that the blind see, the lame walk, the lepers are cleansed, the deaf hear, the dead are raised, the poor have the gospel preached to them. And blessed is he who is not offended because of me.'" (Luke 7:22–23, NKJV).

All I can tell you is that immediately, in that very moment, my mom simply became my mom again. She wasn't someone to be fixed, or a means for proving the power of the gospel. She was just my mom. I brushed her hair, started telling her how much I appreciated her, told her she had done a great job, kissed her forehead and cheek, and fell in love all over again. She looked more peaceful than she had looked in fifteen months. Twenty-four hours later my mom stepped into eternity, and I gave praise and honor to the Lord.

The enemy of my soul had indeed drawn a line in my spirit. He wanted to keep me from continuing to pray for others. But a faithful God spoke about my heart and not about my performance. As a result, I chose to step over that line, and I persist in praying for the sick, broken, and dying. As the apostle Paul wrote, "No temptation has overtaken you except what is common to mankind. And God is faithful; he will not let you be tempted beyond what you can bear. But when you are tempted, he will also provide a way out so that you can endure it" (1 Cor. 10:13).

TRUSTING FOR JUSTICE

Do we really want to experience God's justice? Don't we really want His grace and mercy instead? We have been told by some Bible teachers that we should want God's mercy and grace, not His justice. They explain that:

- Justice is getting what you deserve.

- Mercy is not getting what you deserve.

- Grace is getting what you don't deserve.

Their assumption is that we all deserve hell because we have all sinned and fallen short of the glory of God. Therefore, if God were to apply justice, we would all go to hell. But because Jesus paid the penalty for our sin, we receive mercy and grace through faith in Jesus and thus receive forgiveness, new life, and eternity in heaven.

To this teaching we say a big *yes and amen!* However, we also say if the teaching about justice ends there, we miss a huge part of what God wants to provide for His children here on earth today!

When we come to faith, believe in Jesus as our Savior, and make Him Lord of our lives, we become children of God and coheirs with Jesus. We receive grace and mercy for our sin. Jesus takes the penalty for us, and He ensures that the requirements of a righteous God are met. Justice is served in His death, burial, resurrection, and ascension. This is how justice for salvation is completed.

But now that we are His saved children there is another form of justice that must be recognized and requested. The desire of the Lord's heart is to *make every wrong* (any area that Satan has stolen, killed, or destroyed in our lives) *right* (as the Lord would have it be for us). He has a zealous commitment to do this. His Word says:

> The LORD loves righteousness and *justice; the earth is full* of his unfailing love.
> —PSALM 33:5, EMPHASIS ADDED

> Here is my servant whom I have chosen, the one I love, in whom I delight; I will put my Spirit on him, and he will proclaim *justice to the nations.*

He will not quarrel or cry out; no one will hear his voice in the streets. A bruised reed he will not break, and a smoldering wick he will not snuff out, till he has brought *justice through to victory.*

—MATTHEW 12:18–20, EMPHASIS ADDED

And will not God bring about *justice for his chosen ones,* who cry out to him day and night? Will he keep putting them off? I tell you, *he will see that they get justice,* and quickly. However, when the Son of Man comes, will he find faith *on the earth?*

—LUKE 18:7–8, EMPHASIS ADDED

It can be difficult to believe that God is concerned about justice when our circumstances may seem so unfair. For years Mark denied that he felt cheated out of having two full arms and hands because of his birth defect. It was too painful to admit that God in His wisdom allowed that which He could have easily prevented. It seemed immature and juvenile to feel ripped off, especially when so many others were suffering with much deeper wounds. But as God brought these emotions to the surface, He began to teach us what it meant to trust that He is a God of justice.

What does God's justice look like? Does the restoration of those things God never intended be stolen from us come back to us in the exact form of what was lost? The answer to the latter question is sometimes *yes* and sometimes *no.* The child killed by a drunk driver may resurrect at the scene of the accident when we cry out for life. The loss of a job through false accusation may lead to a more prosperous and fulfilling opportunity.

While God's justice is sometimes immediate and direct, it can also come over time and in indirect ways. Also, it is possible that what is unjust for one brings justice to others. An unexpected death can bring life to many others through organ donation. A devastating disease can result in medical research that brings healing for others. A painful job loss for one can lead to new employment for another.

What we can be assured of is God's commitment to:

- Take what man intends for evil and turning it to our good: "You intended to harm me, but God intended it for good to accomplish what is now being done, the saving of many lives" (Gen. 50:20).

- Bring beauty out of our ashes: "... to comfort all who mourn and provide for those who grieve in Zion—to bestow on them a crown of beauty instead of ashes, the oil of joy instead of mourning, and a garment of praise instead of a spirit of despair. They will be called oaks of righteousness, a planting of the Lord for the display of his splendor" (Isa. 61:2–3).

- Make all things come together for our good: "And we know that in all things God works for the good of those who love him, who

have been called according to his purpose"
(Rom. 8:28).

Over time the truth of Scripture settled into our spirits. We recognized that the character, commission, and commitment of Jesus was (and is) to bring justice *on the earth.* The Bible says, "Your kingdom come...*on earth* as it is in heaven" (Matt. 6:10, NKJV, emphasis added). Again and again the Word talks about God bringing His justice:

> Of the greatness of his government and peace there will be no end. He will reign on David's throne and over his kingdom, establishing and upholding it with *justice* and righteousness from that time on and forever. The zeal of the Lord Almighty will accomplish this.
> —ISAIAH 9:7, EMPHASIS ADDED

> For I, the Lord, love *justice;* I hate robbery...
> —ISAIAH 61:8, EMPHASIS ADDED

> Yet the Lord longs to be gracious to you; therefore he will rise up to show you compassion. For the Lord is a God of *justice.* Blessed are all who wait for him!
> —ISAIAH 30:18, EMPHASIS ADDED

> "But let him who boasts boast of this: that he understands and knows Me, that I am the LORD, who exercises loving kindness, *justice* and righteousness *on earth*, for I delight in these things," declares the LORD.
> —JEREMIAH 9:24, NAS, EMPHASIS ADDED

We must commit ourselves to bringing any area that Satan (the adversary and the accuser) has stolen, killed, or destroyed in our lives to the Lord for a just ruling. The Lord of lords and King of kings will act on our behalf when we bring these areas before Him by faith. Justice is indeed getting what we deserve—*because we have already received His mercy and grace.* We have learned to faithfully cry out for and rest in the promise that justice for those things stolen from us will be addressed and the wrong of Mark's birth defect will be made right. We delight ourselves in the Lord, believing without reservation that He will give us the desires of our hearts regarding His justice!

TRUSTING FOR ANSWERED PRAYERS

In God's kingdom it should be the rule, not the exception, that we receive answers to prayer. When someone comes to church and hears us say, "We love and serve a living God who hears and answers our prayers," they need to see evidence that we truly believe that. If you believe the doctrine that God answers prayer, do you really expect Him to do so? Receiving answers to prayer should be the normal Christian experience.

Often our motivation to pray for others comes from a sense of duty rather than from an expectation to receive. When you go through a season of unanswered prayer and loss of expectation, you may find it helpful to ask yourself these questions:

- Am I ignoring the Holy Spirit (Eph. 4:30)?

- Am I giving legal rights to my enemy
  (Eph. 4:27)?

- Am I experiencing spiritual battle
  (Rev. 12:12; Eph. 6:10–14)?

- Am I praying my own agenda and not His
  (Isa. 55:8–9)?

- Am I thanking Him for the time of
  silence as I continue to ask Him to speak
  (Ps. 119:145–149)?

Scripture says that God's eyes are searching to and fro for a person or a people to whom He can show Himself strong. He is searching over us right now. Let's get His attention and cry out, "Lord, do not pass us by!" Let's pray that:

- It becomes true in our experience that God
  wins and the devil loses (Rom. 16:20).

- We don't break down but we do the breaking
  down (2 Cor. 10:4).

- We are not overtaken by the flood but
  we bubble over and produce His flood
  (John 7:37–38).

- We don't walk around mortally wounded or
  held in captivity, but we bind the wounds
  of the broken and set the captives free
  (Ps. 147:3).

When walking in the promises that our heavenly Father has made to us, we must obey whether we understand or not. We are no longer calling the shots and relating to God on our own terms. If we are to experience the fulfillment of such amazing promises and to receive such precious gifts, we need to *trust God's good intentions* for our lives.

Don't Forget

- When we move ahead of God's timing, we set ourselves up for disappointment because God is still putting things into place. When the fulfillments of His promises come, it will not harm us or our loved ones.

- We sometimes feel emotionally numb toward God because He is using hiddenness to teach us to walk in the Spirit rather than according to our feelings.

- There is purpose in brokenness, and it is to teach us to put our confidence in God and not in our own abilities.

- We can pray for others during times of personal brokenness, but we must keep our focus on the truth of Scripture and not on how we feel.

- Our faith is more important to God than our successes and results.

- We cannot let prayer that isn't answered our way keep us from continuing to pray for ourselves and others.

- When we become children of God, we are qualified to receive justice as coheirs with Christ.

- Because God is zealously committed to making every wrong in our lives right, we are invited to cry out for justice.

- We must be willing to explore why our prayers are not being answered, rather than just wrongly attributing the lack to be on God's side of the requests.

LET'S PRAY

Father, help me to trust You. Slow me down when I start to run ahead of You. Help me to be patient while You put things in place. Strengthen my faith to believe that You are right by my side, even when I don't feel Your presence. God, I know that You make all things work together for good. In Your hands, my brokenness has purpose. I thank You for being a Father who loves to give His children justice. Please repay what the enemy has stolen from me; give back what is rightfully mine. I understand that I can only receive Your justice because Your Son paid the penalty for my sin. I am humbled and grateful. I trust You with my dreams, with my promise, and with my life. Amen.

*How remarkable that we all carry
within us the ability to please God.*

Chapter 8

MAKING GOD SMILE

ARK HAD JUST returned from a 2011 Global Awakening conference in Pennsylvania. As he unpacked his suitcase, he told me of an amazing couple he had met. As mentioned earlier, Mark traveled with Randy Clark in the early nineties and met all kinds of awesome people from around the world. I was happy for him then but felt his connections at that time had little to do with me. That was until he showed me the website of this couple.

The Holy Spirit had powerfully touched Mike and Deena Van't Hul when Randy prayed for them at a conference in 2000. In 2005 Mike and Deena moved their family to China and began to take in disabled orphans. They renovated an abandoned elementary school in Fuzhou China and opened Hidden Treasures Home. As I looked at the pictures of their beautiful children on the Loaves and Fishes International website, tears flowed freely down my face. I said out loud, "I want to go there."

It was now 2013, and we found ourselves holding orphaned babies halfway around the world in the place we had dreamt of. We pinched ourselves to be sure it was true. God had made a way for us to go. We held babies, wrestled with toddlers, played games, sang in Donald Duck voices, worshipped, and prayed. Some of the children were unable to speak, some unable to walk, some autistic, and some blind. The joy that comes from being with children such as these was very familiar to us. The difference was that Jesus was at the center of everything this orphanage did.

THE PUREST OF PRAYERS

One day after morning circle time, a young boy in the classroom asked the teacher assistant a question in Chinese. The assistant was able to speak English and she approached Mark. "An Fu wants to know if he can pray for your arm." We were pleasantly surprised. Of course we were happy to have this precious boy pray. Without hesitation or reservation, An Fu made his way toward Mark on bent legs that made it difficult for him to walk. He held Mark's small arm in both of his hands and prayed these words in very clear English:

> Jesus, Jesus—arm, hand, grow; arm, hand, grow.
> Jesus, heal. Jesus, heal. Thank You, Jesus. Thank
> You, Jesus.

The presence of the Lord permeated the room. We knew we were standing on holy ground. We came home from China with a renewed sense of awe at how God moves in people's hearts. Every day there are prayers for missing body parts at Hidden Treasures Home. It was an atmosphere filled with faith. It was an honor and a joy to be in such a place.

One of our favorite verses in the Bible is Hebrews 11:6: "And without *faith* it is impossible to *please* God, because anyone who comes to him must believe that he exists and that he rewards those who earnestly seek him" (emphasis added).

This verse doesn't say that without *success* it is impossible to please God or without *results* it is impossible to please God. We please our heavenly Father by having faith. When sweet An Fu prayed in faith that Mark's arm would grow out, God was smiling; God was pleased. When by faith Mark let down his guard and allowed this prayer, God was smiling; God was pleased. Faith that steps out in love and takes the risk of praying for others makes God smile. How remarkable that we all carry within us the ability to please God. Scripture says:

> Now faith is confidence in what we hope for and assurance about what we do not see.
>
> —HEBREWS 11:1

We easily believe in what we see, but faith is being confident and assured about what we do not see. We have not seen an arm grow out, but we have faith that it will. How wonderful that this faith does not make our Father shake His head in concern that we have gone off the deep end. This faith makes Him smile because we are assured of what we do not see, as God's Word declares.

Then Jesus told him, "Because you have seen me,
you have believed; blessed are those who have not
seen and yet have believed."

—JOHN 20:29

For you were once darkness, but now you are light
in the Lord. Live as children of light (for the fruit
of the light consists in all goodness, righteousness
and truth) and *find out what pleases the Lord.*

—EPHESIANS 5:8–10, EMPHASIS ADDED

GOD IS PLEASED
WHEN WE RECEIVE

We were excited and a little nervous. "You push the doorbell." "No, you push the doorbell." How did we end up in
northern Idaho, standing on the front porch of Mr. John
Loren Sandford, a man we dearly admired but had no idea
we would ever meet?

I had written John thanking him for allowing us to ref-
erence a quote in our book and to express how he and
his recently departed wife, Paula, had inspired Mark and
me to team teach and minister together. I mentioned that
it would be wonderful to meet him and that perhaps we
could take a detour on our trip out west. We really had
no expectation of that becoming a reality. John's quick
response and invitation to stay at his home surprised us.
We added eight hundred miles to our road trip just to
spend time with this wonderful man and brother in Christ.

Our three days and nights with John were relaxing in
some respects and challenging in others. Between tours
of the town, home-cooked meals, Western movies, and

baseball games on TV, we spent hours before the Lord asking Him to show us anything we needed to know. Early into our visit we shared with John God's promise of a creative miracle and the twenty-year journey of trust. He responded, "When I first saw you two come through the door, the Lord told me He was going to do that, but I wasn't going to mention it until you said something." That was not what we expected to hear, but it was exciting.

The Lord taught us much through John. The first revelation came when Mark shared the story of when his older twin sisters first saw him and how they cried inconsolably. Mark spoke of the inner vow he made to never allow anyone to be disappointed because of him again. He also went on to assure John that he had renounced and broken that vow, and much good had resulted.

Now John spoke. He gently expressed that even though Mark had correctly perceived the lie that his spirit had taken in as an infant, Mark the adult now needed to acknowledge that his understanding of why his sisters cried was incorrect. The inner vow he made put him on constant alert to try to control other people's emotions. He didn't want anyone to ever feel pain. This prevented him from seeing what his sisters' tears really meant. John said, "Mark, your sisters didn't cry because they were disappointed. They cried because they loved you and were sad for you." That thought had never occurred to Mark, and a single tear began to roll down his cheek.

The idea of someone reacting with sadness out of love for him was completely new and tender territory. John explained it was time to open his heart and receive the love he didn't take in as an infant. It was time to renounce control and to realize that people were going to feel emotions regarding his disability. It was a crippling illusion and inappropriate to think that he should try to prevent this. Mark had to allow people to feel emotions for him. He had to permit them to express sorrow *for* him, have joy *for* him, and feel *for and with* him. He had to allow people to feel the way they needed and wished to without controlling.

The next question from John pushed another button in Mark. He asked, "What if God wants to give you an arm and hand just because He loves you, just a good gift from a Father to His son? What if it is not being given to you for the sake of others? What if it is not being given so you'll pray more effectively for others to receive their miracles?"

Mark's response was intense and immediate, "I don't want that; I couldn't handle the guilt. I think the guilt would crush me." With John's fifty-plus years of leading people through inner healing and writing books used around the world on the topic, the word *guilt* waved a big red flag. "Why would you feel guilty, Mark?" he asked. "Aren't you worthy of receiving a gift from your heavenly Father?" Layer by layer the Holy Spirit uncovered other beliefs that Mark didn't even know he held on to. These thoughts were:

- If we receive our promise, and others who see or hear us have not yet received theirs, it will trigger sorrow and grief in them, and they will feel overlooked by God. We would be unhappy and guilt-ridden to have received such a great miracle unless others also receive theirs.

- God will not receive glory because our miracle will cause others to focus on what they do not yet have.

- After we receive our miracle, we must be used by God to pray for others, and they must receive their creative miracles. From our earliest training in praying for the sick, we were taught that God will do *through us* what He has done *to us*. When Mark first traveled with Randy Clark, he would pray for people through the night. We pictured ourselves doing the same.

We came to realize that God may be thinking differently. Receiving ministry from John left us with much to process. We decided to go out to breakfast the next morning to try to sort things through. So over warm plates of eggs, bacon, and pancakes Mark and I talked and explored these new thoughts with each other and with the Lord. We thought it might help to bring up scenarios we had only allowed ourselves to discuss out loud on rare occasions.

We imagined ourselves standing on a stage with Mark's arm and hand fully formed. We could envision people being filled with joy for us over how God had moved. We then asked ourselves, What if people, rather than feeling grieved and overlooked by God because their own circumstances had not yet changed, felt a sense of awe and reverence toward God because of what He did for us. What if no one asked us to pray for them because they were overcome with joy over what had already happened? What if it will be a moment like the one described in Psalm 126:

> When the LORD restored the fortunes of Zion, we were like those who dreamed. Our mouths were filled with laughter, our tongues with songs of joy. *Then it was said among the nations, "The LORD has done great things for them."* The LORD has done great things for us, and we are filled with joy. Restore our fortunes, LORD.... Those who sow with tears will reap with songs of joy. Those who go out weeping, carrying seed to sow, will return with songs of joy, carrying sheaves with him.
> —PSALM 126:1–6, EMPHASIS ADDED

Little by little we came to realize that though we attempted to be selfless in our thinking about future ministry, we had really made this whole thing much too much about us. We had taken control away from God and decided for ourselves what life should look like after the miracle happened based on our past experiences.

The Holy Spirit revealed that it was difficult for us to receive God's unconditional love from Him and others. The condition we had placed on God's gift was that we should be able to give it away or we would crumble in guilt. With much prayer we came to the place of laying down our preconceived notions of what life should be like after the miracle. We laid it at the foot of His wonderful, freeing cross, and chose to take our hands off. We did this by asking God to forgive us for taking control away from Him.

HOW MUCH FAITH DO WE NEED?

When I was a young girl, my mom wore a necklace that intrigued me. It was a clear round capsule, and it contained a single mustard seed. The seed was extremely tiny. My mom told me that she wore the necklace to remind her of the following Bible verse:

> Truly I tell you, if you have faith as small as a mustard seed, you can say to this mountain, "Move from here to there," and it will move. Nothing will be impossible for you.
> —MATTHEW 17:20

If we give our little seed of faith to the maker of heaven and earth, things change, things move, things bow down, things are created! Nothing is impossible for us because nothing is impossible for Him, and He lives in us.

So why is it that even when we apply all the faith we can muster and our faith is placed in Jesus, our mountains seem to stay firmly planted and immovable? We believe the answer to that question is rooted in our expectation and our definition of *movement*.

Matthew 17:20 does not say the mountain will move instantly. We like "instant" answers, but God does not always work that way. We may look at other people and determine that the answers to their prayers have come instantly because we happened to be there the moment the healing took place or the moment the house sale came through. We don't know the emotional preparation that took place before the healing or the amount of renovation that occurred before the sale. In God's economy movement is a process, even movement that appears instantaneous.

Matthew 17:20 also does not say the mountain will move as one large mass. Have you ever played the game Jenga? To set up the game, you make a tower by placing rectangular blocks in a crisscross pattern. The object of the game is to remove a block without causing the tower to tumble. There is a trick to finding the block that is movable. You tap on the ends to discover which ones will slide out of the stack without disrupting the entire structure. Often one block is immovable until the blocks around it are removed.

We have seen God move mountains in a similar way, one block at a time. We speak to the mountain and tell it to move by forgiving someone. Once that block goes, we speak to the mountain and tell it to move by renouncing an ungodly inner vow. Once that block goes, we speak to the mountain again and tell it to move by asking God to heal our current broken relationships. Eventually our mountain moves from here to there, and we have not crumbled in the process.

As We Are Going

After Jesus rose from the dead and before He ascended to heaven, He gave His disciples very specific instructions. Many in the church call this the Great Commission.

> Therefore go and make disciples of all nations, baptizing them in the name of the Father and of the Son and of the Holy Spirit, and teaching them to obey everything I have commanded you. And surely I am with you always, to the very end of the age.
>
> —MATTHEW 28:19–20

The words "therefore go" are literally translated "as you are going." In other words, as we live and go about our everyday lives we are to live out of who we are, with our destinies and promises going with us. We are not to be consumed looking for *the* person(s), *the* place(s), *the* thing(s) that fit with our promises before we serve. God fulfills our destinies and promises *as we go.* Each day lived in obedience to Christ is a day full of faith that pleases Him and holds the probability of our miracles being fulfilled *as we are going!*

This is the faith that makes God smile, the faith that moves mountains. It is faith that steps out in love, that releases control to God, and that is lived out in daily acts of obedience to Christ.

DON'T FORGET

- Faith that steps out in love and takes the risk of praying for others makes God smile.

- It is important to receive gifts from God as unconditional acts of love between a Father and His child and not have preconceived ideas of what God wants to do with the gift.

- Even a tiny seed of faith will move mountains if that faith is placed in God.

- Mountains don't always move instantly or en masse, but often they move gradually, one block at a time, when faith is applied.

- Each day lived in obedience to Christ holds the probability of our promises being fulfilled *as we are going!*

LET'S PRAY

Father, I want to please You, to make You smile. There are times when my faith is no bigger than a mustard seed, but I put my faith in You and know that You will move on my behalf. I know that it pleases You when I pray for others. Help me to have the courage to pray even when my own problems feel overwhelming. May I make You smile today and every day. Amen.

CONCLUSION

A FINAL WORD FROM TAMMY

THIS MORNING WAS no different than most. I woke up before I had to get out of bed and lay there with my body still and my eyes closed. As soon as I felt Mark stirring I reached over and touched his short arm and small hand. I wasn't reaching for the object of a promised miracle. I was reaching for my best friend, my faith partner, and the man God had chosen to be my husband. Unable to imagine being any happier than I felt at that moment, I snuggled closer.

On some mornings my mind begins to plan the day's activities. On other mornings I have thoughts—not prayers but thoughts—that I share with God such as, "Will our miracle happen today? We feel ready. Life will become much busier then."

I don't feel anxious about seeing the promise fulfilled as I did twenty years ago. I feel peaceful and assured. I know that God is smiling and enjoying every one of these still morning moments. The Lord knows He isn't just a miracle worker for Mark and me, but that He is our first love and the author of everything we know to be true and good. Our heavenly Father is as much a part of us as we are of each other.

When the morning does come that I reach over and finally touch our fulfilled promise, Mark will still be my best friend and faith partner, and God will still be our first love. In many ways, things won't be different at all.

A FINAL WORD FROM MARK

I was ministering in one of my favorite countries in Europe, Norway. A man who had been disabled in his knees for thirteen years had just been completely healed—no more pain and fully mobile. I had just left this man dancing in the front row. Before continuing to pray for others, I needed to grab a quick snack—a candy bar and bottled water. I thanked the young teenage girl who was working the refreshment stand and asked her if there was anything I could pray for her about. She started to cry and turned her face away from me. We were alone, and I assured her that it was fine, to not worry about crying, and that I would love to pray for her need.

She gathered herself and said, "My math teacher has been touching and violating me yesterday and today." I said, "Oh, sweetheart, who knows about this, who have you told?" "No one" was her reply. "Not even your parents?" I asked. "I can't tell my dad because he is the pastor of this church, and it would break his heart." I said to her, "Honey, this is the one person you can and must tell. I will go with you."

So there I was sitting on the edge of the stage at one o'clock in the morning in Norway. Everyone was gone except this precious girl, the pastor, and me. As I observed them talking and crying, I saw a loving father embracing his hurting child. Her hurt was now in the light, and based on the response I saw from her father, I knew that even this injustice was going to be healed.

That evening when I laid my head down on the pillow, I asked the Lord to answer a specific prayer: "Lord, You insured that this precious girl would not leave that meeting before receiving the very thing You had on Your heart for her to receive. I ask that from this point forward You would never let anyone in a meeting, a church, or anywhere we minister leave the room before receiving what You have on Your heart for them."

OUR PRAYER FOR YOU

This is our prayer for you, dear reader! We pray that everything God has for you—all the hope, all the encouragement and all the healing God desires you to receive would manifest in your life.

Tammy and I pray:

> *Lord, please make certain that our readers do not close the pages of this book without receiving all that is in Your heart for them to receive. We entrust them into Your loving arms. We do this with the full assurance that You will heal every hurt, provide the way of escape, and fulfill Your precious promises. We seal this prayer in the matchless name of Jesus. Amen.*

SELAH FOR NOW

IN MANY TRANSLATIONS of the Book of Psalms *Selah* occurs more than seventy times. The exact meaning of the word is unknown, but many scholars believed it to be a musical term that means to pause or to reflect. For example, in Psalm 32:5 we read:

> I acknowledged my sin to You and my iniquity I did not hide; I said, "I will confess my transgressions to the Lord"—and You forgave the guilt of my sin. *Selah.*
>
> —NAS

So when we see *Selah*, it means there is a pregnant pause. This pause gives us time to reflect before we move on with the song, music, or play. With peace in our hearts, we must take an *intermission*—a *Selah*. We part with you until our story of promise is further fulfilled. We *Selah* (pause) and *Selah* (reflect).

> God is not a man, that he should lie, not a human being, that he should change his mind. Does he speak and then not act? Does he promise and not fulfill?
>
> —NUMBERS 23:19

NOTES

CHAPTER 1
LEARNING TO HEAR

1. Randy Clark, *Words of Knowledge* (Mechanicsburg, PA: ANGA, 2010), 2.
2. Graham Cooke, *Prophecy & Responsibility: A Journey Into Receiving Revelation and the Process of Godly Communication* (Vacaville, CA: Brilliant Book House, 2010), 80.
3. Ibid., 81.

CHAPTER 2
HOLDING ON TO HOPE

1. Bob Sorge, *The Fire of Delayed Answers* (Canandaigua, NY: Oasis House, 1996), 172.
2. Adel Bestavros, "In Memoriam," http://www.bestavros.net/adel/ (accessed April 2, 2014).
3. Bill Johnson, *How to Overcome Disappointment* (Redding, CA: Sound Wisdom Bethel Church. n.d.), CD.
4. Ibid.
5. Ibid.

CHAPTER 3
EMBRACING YOUR PROMISE

1. Johnson, *How to Overcome Disappointment.*

CHAPTER 4
TREASURING THE UNSEEN

1. Portions of Bob Sorge's testimony were drawn from his teaching "God Could Have Left Job Alone," http://www.youtube.com/watch?v=9FZ5uM_YfB4 (accessed April 2, 2014). Used with permission.

CHAPTER 5
LETTING GO OF CONTROL

1. John Loren and Paula Sandford, The Transformation Series (Coeur d'Alene ID: Elijah House, n.d.), CD.
2. Ibid.

CHAPTER 6
ALLOWING YOURSELF TO FEEL

1. James R. White, "Grief: God's Way of Healing the Heart," http://www.texasstar.net/autumn/grief3.html (accessed April 2, 2014).
2. Ibid.
3. John Loren and Paula Sandford, *God's Power to Change: Healing the Wounded Spirit* (Lake Mary, FL: Charisma House, 2007), 262.

CHAPTER 7
TRUSTING GOD'S INTENTIONS

1. Mark Hendrickson, *Supernatural Provision: Where God Guides, He Provides* (Shippensburg, PA: Destiny Image, 2011), 194.
2. Graham Cooke, *Hiddenness and Manifestation* (Vacaville, CA: Brilliant Book House, 2003), 19.
3. Sorge, *The Fire of Delayed Answers*, 68.

HAND OF
JESUS
MINISTRIES
Healing through His love.

MARK & TAMMY ENDRES

If you would like to invite Mark and Tammy to speak at
your church or ministry event, please contact them at:

info@handofjesus.org